HATHCOCK AND BURKE: THE MARINES' DEADLY DUO

By Robert F. Burgess

𝕾𝖕𝖞𝖌𝖑𝖆𝖘𝖘 𝕻𝖚𝖇𝖑𝖎𝖈𝖆𝖙𝖎𝖔𝖓𝖘

308 W. Marion Street
Chattahoochee, Florida 32324

HATHCOCK AND BURKE:
THE MARINES' DEADLY DUO
By Robert F. Burgess

SPYGLASS PUBLICATIONS, CHATTAHOOCHEE, FLORIDA

A 2020 Paperback Edition
For information address:

Robert F. Burgess
Spyglass Publications
308 West Marion Street
Chattahoochee, Florida 32324

Cover Photo: Marine sniper Carlos Hathcock II
in sitting position to fire. Note size of his Unertl 8x scope.
Courtesy WikiMedia
Cover Design © Robert F. Burgess

Author photo by Charles Harnage Jr.

In memory of David Bennett
A Ranger during the Korean War
An Expert Marksman
He was the best
Here's to you, Pal

This book is also dedicated especially
To you guys who stepped up to the plate
When your country said it needed you.
You are our *real* heroes.

TABLE OF CONTENTS

Foreword: You may have read about legendary Marine snipers Hathcock and Burke before. But in this over 22,000-word book based on actual events, the author puts you right beside them watching the very things that made them legends. Unlike other biographers, he adds answers to details that many never knew at the time. If you fought in Nam you may have wondered at these too. For instance how did the enemy move so easily through the jungle in total darkness? How did they avoid booby traps set by their own people? How did they disappear so quickly? If your buddy was killed in a firefight, why was his body never found?

As you go along with Marine Gunnery Sergeant Carlos Hathcock and Lance Corporal John R. Burke on these legendary missions watch how they unravel various clues in their search for a sniper. After that, you too will know the answers to these long ago mysteries.

This is high-tension vintage action from an author who doesn't mince words and doesn't overlook details of these actual events. After reading this, you will have shared a small bit of their Nam action…in the comfort and safety of your easy chair. But now, perhaps, you will know a bit more about what our veterans went through during this very difficult and unpopular war. Hopefully, you will also appreciate why these veterans deserve every ounce of respect for the terrible sacrifices they made for us. Especially those who like 23-year-old Lance Corporal John R. Burke from Clearwater, Florida gave everything they had to give.

For this read you better wear your flak jacket just in case.

1

From a Grassy Knoll

Vietnam 1967

The small dark-skinned man whose thin clothing was laced with ferns and other camouflaging greenery lay perfectly still beside a log on one of the many surrounding jungle knolls. His long Mosin Nagant rifle rested solidly on a small sniper's pack in front of him. In the half-light he now closed then opened his eyes to peer through his rifle's short 3.5-power scope at the Marine encampment across the gorge.

The sniper had made his way to this position in the dark of night by following a faintly glowing trail on scattered objects along the way. He laid this trail one evening after the Marines had called an end to their day of war and gone to supper. It was made from the mashed-up bodies of many fireflies mixed with a thick waxy plant juice. A smudge of the same bluish-green light on the backs of Vietnamese soldiers' packs enabled them to follow each other backpacking supplies and armaments along the Ho Chi Minh Trail. An army of enemy supply troops carried these necessary supplies from North Vietnam into South Vietnam all night long when no one could see to bother them. During the daylight hours when they would have attracted aerial attacks, they all simply vanished until the dark of night returned. The invading Americans never guessed how they could do it on moonless nights totally in the dark. But they did. The NVA (North Vietnamese Army) officers also used the firefly mix on the palms of their hands to read maps in the dark. Often the NVA troops could then attack and try to over-run the invaders while most of them slept.

It was an old trick. All of their jungle soldiers knew these things. The sniper was an old veteran. He had lived a long time by himself in the jungle. He knew what it took to survive there.

From long experience he had been in his shooting place an hour before first light. He knew that shortly after first light early morning habits of the foreign devils would bring him a target; hopefully the one he sought. But as always he would take whatever good fortune sent his way.

Across the gorge from the enemy sniper the view from one of the carefully concealed Marine sniper hides on a projection of Hill 55, thirty miles southwest of Da Nang, was spectacular. Far beyond the sandbag bunkers and concertina wire with its trip flares and Claymore mines was a mottled green world of jungle-covered knolls, scattered villages, glittering rice patties and a winding shallow waterway. The convoluted grassy knolls were known to sometimes hide enemy snipers.

Following first light the lowlands shimmered in a combination of bluish jungle haze and the columns of rising gray smoke of village cooking fires. What drifted up to the Marines atop their heavily guarded sniper training base were the sounds and smells of the jungle country below them.

What interested the sniper on the knoll, however, were the gradually appearing dim gray outlines of the sandbagged fortification on the hill. Through his rifle scope he saw movement. Anticipating where that movement was going he dug in his left sandal toe to move his aim slightly to the right where some sandbags dipped lower. As expected a dark figure with a tan towel over his shoulder paused momentarily as he reached up to open the door to a latrine.

The sniper's finger tightened on his trigger. The sudden sharp bark of his Mosin-Nagant rifle echoed and re-echoed across the still valley.

The sniper did not look through his rifle scope again. He

knew what he would see. Before the machine guns began their chatter, he picked up his brass and faded into the mists down the back side of the knoll.

2

Sniper vs Sniper

In the last few weeks, U.S. Marine Captain Jim Land had grown gradually more alarmed when he realized that enemy snipers were taking more casualties than ever from his base. The Marines always responded in their direction with a heavy peppering of .50-caliber machinegun fire but no one knew if it ever found its target. Why were the Marines getting more harassment? Land didn't have to wonder about that very long. Intel reported that they had captured a Vietnamese woman who talked freely...even bragged about the reason why. She told them that a squad of top North Vietnamese Army snipers had been dispatched to find and kill a particularly troublesome Yankee sniper they called, *Long Tra'ng* meaning White Feather. A large ransom would be paid any one of their soldiers who could either capture or kill this much-hated Marine sniper. All they knew was that he came from Hill 55 so they stepped up their sniper action there.

The man they wanted everyone knew was gunny Carlos Hathcock. This slim, wiry Arkansas sharpshooter had already taken out so many of their kind and left his calling card of a single white feather that he was fast becoming a legend. Apparently the enemy figured that taking pot shots at any of the soldiers on Hill 55 would eventually catch the man they most wanted.

When Carlos' Marine buddies heard this they all started wearing white feathers in their jungle hats. "Bring 'em on," they shouted. "We're all *Long Tra'ngs!*"

Hathcock just grinned when he saw them do that. Captain Land gave their well-liked gunny a head's up on the situation.

Carlos liked the idea that he was a magnet for those hamburgers. If his being there was drawing them to him, he was quick to see it as a chance for him and his partner, Johnny Burke to go into the bush for a few days to see if they could target any of these nuisances.

Both men kept their gear ready to go at a moment's notice. Carlos took special care of his match-conditioned .30-06 Springfield caliber, Model-70 Winchester fitted to a glass-bedded Monte Carlo-style stock. It was his carefully sighted in fine-tuned baby. Atop it was carefully mounted a long eight-power Unertl scope.

When the early morning enemy sniper shot and killed one of their men just steps away from their hooch, that was all the more reason they needed to go. The team of Hathcock and Burke slipped out long before dawn the next morning and silently disappeared into the misty jungle to go sniper hunting. Before leaving they talked to their machine-gunners to learn which knoll they thought he had fired from.

As it grew light the two camouflaged snipers with their slotted clothes now hidden in fresh greenery slowly worked their way around a side of the target knoll looking for some sign of disturbance. Their grease-painted faces were darkened with the green and black of their jungle make-up. Their communication was by hand signals.

On the backside of the knoll the grass still soaked from the night's shower bore signs of a large object having passed downhill that way. If it wasn't a rock ape or some other night creature both men figured it was the sniper.

They followed the mashed down grass to the water's edge of a narrow meandering stream. There they paused to look closely at the grass. Was it flattened widely along the edges of the waterway as though an animal had made the disturbance as it drank, leaving marks in the mud where his feet held him?

No. There were no prints. The animal…or man had gone straight into the water. The snipers waded in too. Feeling the current pushing them downstream they grinned at each other. Both thought much the same thing. What a clever way to disappear from where you were by floating off into the jungle somewhere.

But how far, and where? As they floated along Carlos motioned to Johnny. Their left arms balanced their rifles and small sniper packs on their left shoulders. Hathcock pointed to both grassy stream banks and put his pointer finger under his eye.

Burke nodded.

They both lost track of the time as they drifted downstream pausing now and then to look closely at disturbances along its banks. No signs suggested they were made by a human.

The two had drifted for maybe a kilometer when suddenly they saw an inch-thick green sapling whose upper half had been broken and bent down to the ground.

Both snipers knew that was unnatural. It was a VC marker. They had seen that kind of thing before. The VC left signs behind them so their own people knew there was a booby trap or tunnel opening nearby. A folded leaf pierced by a bent twig, a pile of stones, a forked stick in the ground with a pointer stick in its fork; anything that looked unnatural could be a marker.

What did this one mark? A way to disappear into their complex tunnel system…or a hidden grenade in a pop can with its pin pulled halfway until someone touched the mud-buried copper wire as they climbed out of the stream?

Hathcock and Burke took their time checking it out. They found nothing. Hathcock looked carefully at the trunk of the broken young tree and saw no nick of a blade. It appeared that it had been pushed over until it broke. But then he noticed something else on the trunk of the sapling. He looked closer and saw that a waxy substance had been smeared on its trunk.

Then he knew. He pointed it out to Burke and he nodded. This was a marker alright. One someone only saw at night by the bluish green glow of the firefly luminescence. The guy could find this place even in the dark! Talk about clever thought Hathcock.

They looked for matted grass and saw what they thought were indications that whoever had gone that way had made an effort to fluff up the grass behind him…. Or was that done that way on purpose?

That thought bothered Hathcock. A smart tracker might see that ruse as another way to draw in anyone smart enough to follow him. If that was the case then they might be going into a trap.

Once out of water they paused long enough to sip water from their canteens, then they separated a safe distance from each other and went into their worm mode. With Hathcock leading and Burke three paces to his left rear, they crawled slowly in the direction they were being led by the slightly disturbed green grass still dripping with nighttime rain.

They moved slowly enough not to disturb the surrounding bird life and other natural insect sounds of the jungle. They stopped and paused often, listening to any and all sounds they heard. So far all they heard was the continual buzzing sound of the under-story insects.

Both men were sweating heavily from the sweltering jungle humidity and they were constantly being bitten by everything the ground cover had to offer. This included tiny red-bugs smaller than a skin pore that went into your pore thirsting for blood. Then came ticks of all sizes ranging from the seed tick smaller than an apple seed to those that swelled up larger than a pea when they filled with your blood. Snatch one of them out of your armpit instead of singing him with a cigarette or match and he left you the gift of his head buried deep in your hide. Days later if not treated you had a serious infection there. Along with these guys you had large hairy red ants with pliers for pinchers, and three-inch millipedes whose bite felt like a jab from a red hot poker. Whatever decided to feast on them, snipers were trained to ignore it.

Neither man had stopped to rid themselves of the blood-sucking leeches that were now hitchhiking with them, happily sampling the fresh new blood they enjoyed as they dipped into warm recesses under the men's armpits; in their crotches and other body orifices. Later the soldiers scraped off their slimy swollen blood-fattened bodies and squashed them in the comfort of their hooch, leaving huge splotches of their own blood on the floor. All bites from these critters got treated properly when they had the time and the meds, but in the bush they couldn't even slap the mosquitoes that feasted on them.

As the two snipers crawled, they realized the faint grass trail they followed was gradually rising. It seemed to be leading them toward a small clearing ahead. Both snipers approached this area with much more caution. Their movements now were more snail-like. Still, some birds that had been feeding in the grass ahead of them, flushed at their arrival, fluttering up noisily and disappearing overhead.

Before they reached the clearing Carlos slipped out a small pair of binoculars to see if he could spot anything ahead.

Peering low through a patch of leafy green long-stemmed Nandina, he saw that the clearing was in front of a steep grassy shoulder of the hill. What interested him was what appeared to be netting that draped down the front of the hill with various kinds of greenery threaded through it. From a distance it was perfect camouflage for anything behind it. As best he could tell it appeared to hide the opening of a small cave. It could be the opening to one of their tunnel systems.

In front of this place the grass looked pressed down. Everything about it looked odd. It was a little too obvious as though someone wanted it to be seen. Carlos suspected a trap. The sniper was probably somewhere else high on the hill opposite the clearing just waiting for any trackers to approach that poorly hidden cave.

Then he remembered the fluttering of the birds. "Damn..." he thought. He looked more carefully at the ground they were crawling over and saw a scattering of rice and seeds that didn't belong there. *"He already knows we're here!"* Carlos shook his head and signaled Burke they should pull back.

The two reversed themselves and left the track they had been following. Hathcock made a slicing move with his hand near his cheek. He wanted them to circle the clearing and go up the hill toward the ridge. The sun was already lower to the west. That would put it behind them on their right. They had to be extra careful now.

High up the hill on the opposite side of the clearing the man they were looking for already sensed that someone was there. Burrowed down in the grass, lying well-camouflaged in a hide he had made long ago the birds had told him a tracker was on his trail and close to his trap. He peered through his rifle scope searching the far end of the clearing he had seeded, looking carefully and incrementally through the long-stemmed Heavenly Bamboo there looking for any movement that would betray his tracker.

He had killed trackers there before. Most never even saw his poorly camouflaged cave. They were what he called 'greenies.' As soon as they stopped to ponder the clearing they were already in his kill zone. Their bodies were never found. They were the "disappeared." What these foreign devils didn't know was that the Vietnamese fighters made a habit of hiding enemy bodies in their labyrinth of underground tunnels, just to frustrate those who would come looking for them. General Giap had taught them well how to mess with their heads. It was all part of their bag of tricks. The two trackers the sniper had shot were plastered into the side wall of his easily dug red clay cave.

As the sniper watched for movement, he began to think that maybe this visitor was not as green as the two before him. If this tracker suspected a trap, what would he do? The sniper lifted his head from his riflescope, squinted into the setting sun and looked toward the densely covered ridge high and to his left.

Hathcock and Burke were a long ways from that ridge because they were currently trying to slither their way through a tangle of the worse kind of thorny vines they had ever seen. The damn things were light green and thick as a middle finger with heavy barbs every few inches. What made them especially treacherous was that they snaked all through the undergrowth and if you pulled at them the movement shook everything.

All they could do was use their K-bar knives that they kept razor sharp to carve their way through the worse of them. It took an hour just to navigate that barbed-wire batch. They were almost through them when Burke raised his rump to get over one that had its barbs aimed at his private parts.

The sudden jerky movement instantly was caught by the skilled sniper who had been running his squinted eyes back and forth over the distant greenery looking for precisely that – movement on that still green wall.

The explosion of sound as his rifle fired instantly shattered the afternoon silence. The sniper's slug slammed Burke to the ground where his jaws clamped down hard on his lower lip to keep from screaming.

As he felt the pain and the sudden rush of blood pouring hotly down his backside it made him so mad he wanted to swear loud and clear…but he didn't.

"*Jesus!*" he screamed in his head, "*In my ass for Christ sake!*"

Hathcock looked back; saw the situation and immediately clamped his hand over Burke's mouth. The look in Burke's eyes was total astonishment. "*What the hell?*" But what really baffled Burke was Carlos grinning at him… Grinning like a baboon…his own buddy…grinning at him bleeding to death from being shot in the ass for Christ sake!

Wiry Hathcock bent close to whisper in Burke's ear but almost choked he wanted to laugh out loud so bad…. "*Whoa*

Buddy...don't move....you're okay... it's just your canteen... bullet hit your canteen, not you!"

"Huh?" Burke felt back. The bottom of his canteen had been blown away...his fingers came back wet not bloody. *Oh! Thank God!* He tried to calm his hammering heart and his heavy breathing.

They finally crawled out of the vines and managed to work their way through some larger trees that didn't move when they were touched. Now, however, they were closer to the brow of the hill and knew they might be seen as moving silhouettes. The one thing going for them was that the sniper would have to squint into the sunlight when he looked for them.

The sniper wasn't sure if he had hit a tracker or if he had put a slug into a wild animal. If it were a pig or a rock ape he knew the animal would have screamed or squealed and thrashed around...but since neither happened, he had either killed whatever it was...or it was a human who had not screamed and was more dangerous than ever now.

Very carefully the sniper adapted a sitting position with his Mosin Nagent, scanning slowly along the brightly lit rim of the ridge opposite him.

Suddenly he saw movement. Instantly his cross-hairs found the target. His finger tightened...

After that he never heard, nor knew what followed.... He wasn't even aware that everything went black....

When Hathcock glimpsed the sudden glitter of sun on glass he jerked up his rifle and fired.

After the shot he looked through his scope and saw the reflex flopping of the man's body. They waited for a while to be sure it was over then slowly worked their way down to the sniper's hide.

The body was on its back. He was shot in the head. It had blown off the rifle's short scope.

Burke picked it up and looked at it. He was speechless as he handed it to Hathcock.

22

All the lenses had been blown out. The bullet had passed straight through the barrel of the scope and into the sniper' eye!

A shiver ran through Hathcock. *The only reason he was still alive was because his trigger finger had been one millisecond faster than the man who had found him in his scope!*

3

Best of the Best

Camp Perry, Ohio, August 26, 1965. Second and Final Day of the National High Power Rifle Championship – the Wimbledon Cup

Imagine a firing range 1,000 yards long. That is ten football fields laid end-to-end. Now imagine that you are shooting at a target at the other *end of those ten* football fields. Inside that 50-inch target are concentric circles of white and black. What everyone aims for is the dead center of that target – the 20-inch 5-point circle of black. Sighting that bull's-eye through a riflescope from a thousand yards away it looks the size of a pinhead.

Putting your shots inside that inner ring was the goal of a select group of finalist shooters on April 26, 1965. To make this especially difficult the cross wind at the range that day was blowing so hard that a bullet fired at the target would move to the right experts said *almost sixteen feet!*

That was the kind of challenge for the final twenty men who now lay prone on their line mats with their weapons, cartridges, notes and spotting gear. Ten of them had bolt-action rifles; ten had semi-automatic weapons and all of them had competed and won shooting competitions that led to this final big one. They were all considered the best of the best. But only one of them would come out of this competition between expert marksmen with the title of "The best shot in America." He alone would be the winner of the distinguished Wimbledon Cup.

The competition began the day before with 2,600

contestants. Each had been given 10 rounds and ten minutes to fire them. Only 20 survived the cut. And of those, the only remaining contestants firing bolt-action rifles were Marines Carlos Hathcock and a Sergeant named Danny Sanchez.

Hathcock tried to calm himself as he lay prone on his mat with his rifle beside his spotting scope. Under a small hand towel to his right were the rounds he would fire. Beside them were his sweep hand wristwatch and his notebook containing all of his previous observations on how he had to sight his rifle according to various conditions.

Tension had his stomach in a knot. To take his mind off it he leaned to his left and looked through his spotting scope down his lane of the firing range.

Large red pennants along the sides of the range snapped briskly in the wind. It was gusty. One moment the flags streamed out, the next they fell as the wind lulled. He noticed too that the mirage created by heat waves moved from left to right the stronger the wind blew. By his calculations from the data in his notebook, he would hold 14 minutes to the left to compensate for the wind during a lull. He had decided, "That's when I'll fire, when the flag falls in a lull."

He reached up to the knob on the side of his scope that corrected for right and left sightings and carefully counted off 14 clicks that moved the fine crossed wires inside his scope. It now corrected for the lulled wind to hopefully put his shot directly into the tiny black bull's-eye.

After each firing all targets would be lowered into the pits where officials judged the hits and then were lifted again. Pit attendants would then relay the position of that hit or miss to everyone by lifting a 5-foot-long pole with a 20-inch diameter disk painted red on one side and white on the other. If the shot missed the entire target the red marker moved across it from left to right. The same red disk signaled other hits in various positions but the coveted hit dead center in the smallest black circle got the white marker held over that bull's-eye.

Each contestant would be given three minutes to fire one round. The second hand of his watch near his right hand had to be watched carefully. The tension made 23-year-old Carlos breathe faster than usual. He tried to control it. He had done it before. The rifle in his hands felt so familiar to him that it was more like an extension of his arms, as though it was part of him. It had always been that way.

Born on May 20, 1942 Carlos Norman Hathcock II grew up first in rural Arkansas and later in rural Louisiana. The family was not well off. His father had brought him a World War II souvenir German Mauser when he came home from World War II. As a skinny little boy he could hardly drag the heavy rifle with its plugged barrel around outdoors where he used it to play shooting Indians.

In time he and his mother went to live with his Grandmother. On his eighth birthday they gave him a Sears, Roebuck and Co. J. C. Higgins .22 Caliber bolt action single shot rifle. He had wanted one so badly that he was overjoyed with this wonderful gift. Now he spent all of his spare time in the woods keeping the family well stocked in squirrels and swamp rabbits. That's where he learned to shoot so well. He would choose a hide near a hickory tree and pick off the squirrels one-by-one. He never approached the tree until he got them all. He tried never to hit them where it damaged the meat. He always had the patience to wait until just the right moment before he fired. The boy prided himself in making only head shots.

As his father had gone into the service, when Carlos was seventeen years old in 1959, he joined the U.S. Marine Corps. It did not take the Marines long to see that this youngster was a remarkably fine marksman. They swiftly trained him in shooting military rifles on their firing ranges. He loved every bit of it. He made copious entries about what he learned in his small notebook and marveled that they were actually paying him to do what he liked best.

In no time he was competing in various military shooting

competitions and winning one after another for the Marine Corps. Having bested all of the other outstanding shooters he was now about to compete for top gun in the most important shooting competition of all – the Wimbledon Cup Challenge.

An announcement came over the public address system saying that the finalists would now begin their prep time.

Carlos got into his customary prone position with the leather rifle sling in its customary half twist around his left forearm, cinching everything up tight as he brought his eye in line with his scope, using his toes to properly position himself so that the tiny black dot of the bull's eye rested atop the center of his rifle's wire cross hairs.

Now he calmed his breathing until he felt good about everything.

Then the announcement over the PA again: "Gentleman, your prep time has ended."

A band played. The music swelled and replaced the normal buzz of the crowd.

Then once again the metallic sound of the speaker addressed them.

"Gentlemen, you may load one round."

Carlos opened his bolt. He reached over, lifted a corner of his towel and picked up a shiny long brass cartridge. Carefully and smoothly he slipped the .300 Winchester 176-grain Magnum shell into his rifle chamber, then closed and locked his bolt.

Slowly and distinctly the official's voice sounded again. It told them that when the targets came out of the pits that they had three minutes to fire one round.

The 20 targets down range appeared. Carlos noted the position of his second hand. Out of the corner of his eye he watched the range flags near the targets. They stayed out and fluttering.

His fingertip lay on the curve of his trigger. The second hand on his wristwatch was ticking around for its second time. He tried to calm his breathing. A bead of sweat ran down his brow. He opened and closed his eyes. When he looked the second time the sight picture had not changed. He was still centered with the black dot atop the crossed wires. Just before his second hand reached two minutes, the flags fell.

Carlos squeezed off his shot.

He leaned over and looked for his hit in his spotter scope but it told him nothing. He opened his bolt and waited.

At the three minute marker the public address system voice told them to cease fire.

As pit officials checked the results minutes passed, then all the targets moved in unison halfway out of the pits and paused.

The announcer said they would now disk all misses. The targets rose into position. There were no misses. The on-lookers applauded. Then began a series of disking in which the official markers gradually reached the targets' inner circles. One-by-one those who missed hitting within that small central bull's-eye were out of the competition.

Each competitor who had failed to hit the mark stood up, gathered their gear and retired from the field. Each was met by a round of applause for their ability to have achieved this high degree of proficiency. Carlos knew why they had missed – the wind had been the culprit. They had failed to take that into full consideration and had fired too quickly while the banners still fluttered.

Then the announcer told the crowd they would now disk all 5s meaning the small inner circle of black. Only one target rose out of the pit with a white spotter centered in it. It was his. Carlos breathed a sigh of relief.

He got in position for the next round. Thirteen others had survived the cut. The announcer told them to reload and the performance continued. This time six shooters remained. Sanchez, who had kept up with Carlos, was one of them.

Behind them the spectators and the band celebrated their status in music and applause but Carlos no longer heard them. He was totally focused on the task ahead. He felt good about everything. He knew his luck would hold as long as he held onto that 14-click correction. He counted on the wind dropping to nothing within those three minutes so he could fire. If the wind didn't drop off within those three minutes he didn't dare think about that.

He looked down-range at the moving mirage. It seemed that the wind had intensified. He hoped that wasn't true. Only two competitors remained and Sergeant Sanchez was one of them.

The tension was building in Carlos now. His stomach was knotting up. He wiped his brow. He checked his spotting scope again and saw the flags fluttering strongly.

Then the sharp loud voice over the PA system came on: "Gentlemen, you may load one round."

Carlos took the last round from under his towel. Smoothly he chambered it and locked down the bolt. Then he went into his position and sighted in.

The three targets simultaneously appeared from their pits.

He looked at the sweep hand on his watch. "*Three minutes,*" he heard repeatedly in his head.

The cross-hairs firmed up with the pinhead spot centered atop it.

The flags still briskly fluttered. He held his breath without realizing it. Finally, he let it out. "*Watch it…watch it…*" A red range flag sagged…"

"*Boom!*" came a sharp report as the man beside him fired.

Out of the corner of his eye Carlos saw the flag burst out in renewed speed.

He looked at his watch. *Its sweep hand was starting around for its third and last time!*

The range flag was still outstretched and rippling.

Hathcock's heart hammered. *Forty-five seconds now.*

"*Boom!*" someone else fired.

The flag still kicked. *Thirty seconds left! Now twenty…*The flag dipped. Carlos dug in his toe and shifted his sight a hair more up-wind on the black circle. In the last remaining five seconds he fired…. The range flag was still slightly fluttering.

"*Cease fire. Cease fire,*" blared the loud speaker.

Minutes later his two competitors' targets lifted out of the pits. Both shooters had hit their targets three inches to the right of the black disk.

Then came the announcement:

"Ladies and Gentleman we will now disk the score of the 1965 National Champion, Marine Corporal Carlos N. Hathcock II of New Bern, Carolina." The voice was drowned out by loud cheering and band music but Carlos was not aware of it. He stared through his spotting scope at the target to see where he had hit. The disk rose up over the small black bull's eye. As it moved aside, Hathcock saw a white spot four inches in from the edge of the black.

His slight sight change before the wind fell off had paid off.

He had won the 1000-yard National High Power Rifle championship by four inches!

4

The Deadly Duo

Vietnam 1967

Rolling over on his cot and looking at his hooch buddy Johnny Burke who had just run a patch through the barrel of his Winchester for the umpteenth time, Carlos Hathcock said, "Johnny Boy, it's about time for us to go get us some hamburgers."

Twenty-three-year-old boyishly handsome John R. Burke broke out in a wide smile as though his Clearwater, Florida high school basketball coach had just ordered him into a game and told him to shoot as many baskets as he could for good old Clearwater High. "I hear you," he grinned. "Old Betsy here is just itching to go." He patted his sniper rifle affectionately.

On his second Vietnam hitch on Hill 55 where his sniper school was, U.S. Marine Gunnery Sergeant Carlos Hathcock didn't want to waste any time. He had teamed up with his old buddy Lance Corporal John R. Burke to see what kind of trouble they could raise in Elephant Valley, which was reported to be swarming with enemy activity.

The valley had a history of its own. Southeast of the Dong Den mountain peak, foot-hills drop down to a flat L-shaped valley comprised mostly of checkerboard rice paddies nourished by a serpentine river backed by jungle. Through this flattened gateway the enemy moved both supplies and military forces. In 1965 Marines encamped on the lower jungle-covered ridges of the main mountain were surprised to hear trumpeting from a group of eight elephants loaded with heavy cannons for the enemy. Afterward the Marines called that place Elephant Valley. It was continually used as a main supply route by the enemy Hathcock called *hamburgers*.

"Enemy troops are building strength in that area and anything you can do to disrupt them will be to our advantage," Intel told the snipers.

So Sergeant Hathcock arranged with Intel to take a two-man sniper team into the valley area using artillery for cover fire if they needed it.

"It's almost time," said Hathcock. "We might as well take off. We don't want to keep those hamburgers waiting."

Both Marines would be traveling light as usual, Hathcock carrying a bandoleer of 84 matched grade 30.06 full metal jacketed rounds of ammo, his K-bar knife, a .45 pistol, compass and map, two canteens and a handful of C-Rations with peanut butter and jelly cheese crackers.

Besides his sniper rifle similar to Carlos's Winchester 70 with a scope, Burke brought along an M-14 rifle, binoculars, a radio, canteens, C-Rations and a high-powered spotting scope.

At the LZ they joined up with a squad that was taking a chopper off Hill 55 to go on patrol in that area. The chopper put them down in a clearing. Burke and Hathcock stuck with the patrol until they entered Elephant Valley, then they cut out on their own stopping periodically to watch their back trail to see if anyone had followed them. After that they cut cross-country to the heavy jungle tree line along one side of the valley.

First they established an escape route then they picked their shooting positions, making sure they were well covered with dense vegetation and had a good view in front of their hide just as the sun set sending rainbows of vivid colors across the valley.

In front of them was an open area checkered with berms and rice paddies. These berms served as soil dikes that cut the paddies into squares. One of these dirt levees stuck up out of the water a good two feet high and ran parallel to their position. It was broad enough to serve as a dry pathway across the rice paddies.

Hathcock and Burke were about 700 yards from it or the length of seven football fields end-to-end. A distance just right for them to zero in on any activity along that pathway.

Beyond that land bridge about 3000 feet of more rice fields continued until they ended at a long low tree line of mostly bamboo and palms where the rice farmers lived.

Without a word only hand gestures Burke and Hathcock prepared themselves for the night. As it grew dark the usual insects and animal life sounded off around them. From habit the two of them took turns catnapping. While one slept the other stayed on watch. And then it was the other's turn to nap.

When dawn finally came both of them were wide-awake and ready to do some hunting. Dawn and evening were the two times best suited for hunting the VC because that's when they came out of their tunnels or went back into them for the day.

As the sun rose higher red and hot behind them it dispelled the fog of the valley.

Before long the two snipers heard commotion on the trail below them. As they watched, a whole company of North Vietnamese Army regulars appeared. There were about eighty soldiers. As the snipers anticipated the army contingent stretched out along the narrow berm path across the rice paddies directly in front of them.

They appeared in a hurry. Since this was a relatively open area obviously they were anxious to get across the rice paddies as quickly as they could rather than taking the longer, slower route across the foothills of the mountain in the background.

The snipers knew you don't see this large of a group out so long in the daylight. Normally by this time they would have been out of sight in their tunnels. For this reason alone they were moving as swiftly as they could to get to wherever they were going. The narrow path was a bottleneck that slowed them down now.

In 1966 the NVA had switched the color of their uniforms from tan to dark olive green. They all wore small round helmets atop their heads and all carried Russian Kalashnikov rifles. This was the kind of target snipers only dreamed about because there were so many easy targets and so unlikely that the snipers would be spotted from their complicated hides. It was easy to pick out the officers because they were the ones carrying the side arms. On both sides they were always the first targets. After that came the radiomen who were easy to spot because they always stayed close to their commanders.

Normally the routine would have been to call in the artillery. But that would have scattered them into the jungle where they would have been more difficult to dig out.

It was a perfect day for sniping. No mirages, no wind, no mist.

Hathcock whispered to Burke. "I'll take the officer at the head of the column. You take the one in the rear." Burke nodded.

Both targets dropped at the twin *ka-pows* of their rifles!

Carlos picked off one of the soldiers as the entire company made one wild leap to the only cover in sight – that long raised earthen dike. The side off the path was stagnant rice paddy water. The entire company splashed into it and put the birm between them and what they suspected was an enemy patrol.

Eventually the soldiers began popping their heads up over the dike. All along the dike it was like shooting clay pigeons at a carnival. One of the soldiers jumped up and with his arms and legs windmilling through the water he tried to make it to the river. Hathcock dropped him in mid-floundering before he took half a dozen steps.

When they saw their comrades literally losing their heads when they popped up over the levy the rest of them wisely kept their heads down

They apparently had neither radio nor machineguns to respond to the snipers' fire, or to call for other RVA soldiers to back them up. But these were the misfortunes of war. These soldiers were the enemy. These were the enemy soldiers who relished the idea of capturing any of our soldiers alive because they could torture them all night long and keep our troops in mental agony hearing their tortured screams. These were the Vietnamese soldiers from the north trained to shoot and burn villages of these simple rice-growing people in South Vietnam in order to force them to make their children carry their supplies, or to provide them with food. And it was these NVA soldiers who when Stalker's patrol rewarded a five-year-old Vietnamese girl with some candy and a can of C-rations because she helped the team uncover mines, a high-ranking North Vietnamese army officer who saw her with these treats called her and her parents before the villagers, then shot her parents and chopped off the little girl's left hand as a warning to the other villagers. Such was the face of our enemy in Vietnam, the very same enemy that was now receiving a small measure of payback for a few of their many crimes against humanity. This payback was being meted out by just two sharp-shooting U.S. Marines trained to combat the devilish enemy in the only way they knew how to do it: by treating them as merciless as they treated us. All of that and all of this is why veterans never forget the horror of war; why they never talk about what they had to do to stay alive day after day in this kind of hell. And why they never forgot their comrades who shared the same hell that they all lived or died through together. This too is why politicians who were never combat soldiers are always the ones most eager to go to war.

But it was time for Burke and Hathcock to move before they were detected. They low-crawled a couple hundred feet to their left and once again burrowed into the underbrush for their hides.

Now it turned into a deadly game of jack-in-the-box,

waiting to see along that long levee line where and when the next target got curious or brave enough to pop up his head to look around. If he looked and ducked fast he might be safe. But if he looked longer than he intended, one or the other of the snipers popped him off.

Eventually, the heat of the day bore down on the survivors behind the dike. Slowly but surely they began to dehydrate in the heat. And certainly they were thirsty. If they drank any of the water in the paddy they would surely come down with severe stomach cramps and diarrhea since Vietnamese rice farmers used human waste for their fertilizer.

Since no help came to that trapped enemy company what were their options? If they stayed low behind the dike maybe they could crawl single file slowly but surely in the direction they had to go. Or would it make more sense to stay where they were until nightfall and then in the cover of darkness get back on that dike and run for it? If they couldn't be seen, they couldn't be shot. Also, at night the besieged soldiers could instantly see the muzzle flashes of the snipers and by using the birm to protect them they could send a massive volley of fire at the Marines.

These thoughts had to have gone through their minds. Staying where they were until dark and firing at the muzzle flashes seemed far the best idea.

Except that Hathcock and Burke had considered those possibilities too, realizing that each shot they fired after dark would draw intense enemy fire their way. How could they counter that?

"We'll deal with that problem when we come to it," thought Hathcock. Meanwhile it was snap-shooting-clay-pigeon-day in the shooting gallery.

Obviously the two snipers had the enemy completely pinned down. Now it was a waiting game.

Late in the afternoon when there had been no shots fired for a couple hours one brave NVA raised his head and neither sniper fired. He looked around and one could almost guess what he was saying to his comrades hunkered down in the stinking water near the slowly bloating smelly bodies of their dead comrades.

"I think they have gone," he said. "I think they have left. Look!" He stood up and waved his arms foolishly, showing off to his buddies.

Two other heads popped up and the men began to stand up beside them showing how brave they were too.

As they did the snipers fired. The three NVA lost their lives. After that there wasn't a chance of anyone else looking up over that dike for anything in the world. They had learned their lesson quickly.

Everyone hunkered down and waited for the darkness of night.

"They probably think they will have a chance," said Hathcock, "but we'll take care of that."

Nothing happened and darkness soon came on. When it did the snipers directed artillery to keep the skies over the valley as bright as possible with 105mm flares.

Each of these blazed like a miniature sun. As each set of flares burned out trailing smoke behind them, a new set lit up the world. This went on all night long. Meanwhile the snipers alternated taking catnaps, one or the other of them would fire a round over the dike once an hour to let the hamburgers know they were still there.

Dawn broke with temperatures rising with the sun until it was hotter than ever. By 1000 it was at least 100 degrees.

The snipers saw sporadic movements but had no way to figure what they were doing.

When eight of the soldiers suddenly jumped up and started running toward the tree line firing their AK-47s and screaming at the top of their lungs the snipers knew that one of their officers had ordered this charge. What amused them was that they were yelling and shooting at the wrong area of the tree line. They were about 45 degrees off and Hathcock and Burke took down six of them with no problem at all because they were trying to run through knee-deep water. It was like a charge in slow-motion.

The dike was 700 yards from the tree line and with them going slow it was just a matter of picking what target you wanted to take out.

When the two remaining attackers saw what happened to their comrades they quickly turned around and ran back to the dike. The survivors huddled in the by now very hot paddy water on the other side. Hathcock nailed one of them before he got over the dike so half of him was still exposed while his head and shoulders were in the rice paddy water.

The two snipers changed position again, following the tree line around the side of the valley hoping to flank the company hiding behind the dike. But they were not able to go far enough to get a look at the flank of the NVA hiders. Again it began to get dark and the temperatures fell. A fog moved into the valley. If there was any time that the soldiers felt they might have a chance to get away, now was that time with the fog beginning to take away the snipers' visibility. Still, not one of the NVA tried to escape.

Once more five of the soldiers from behind the dike jumped up and tried to run to the tree line charging and screaming and firing their weapons. But once again they went in the wrong direction. The snipers took their toll of those five.

On the second night the snipers decided to hold off on using the flares and see if the darkness would tempt the soldiers into the open. So they waited a couple of hours and when the miniature sun once again lit up the sky there they were like deer frozen in the headlights. The snipers took out that group in a hurry. This kind of thing went on for the rest of the night until the besieged soldiers stopped trying to make a break.

Through the hot and humid afternoon the snipers took turns dozing. That afternoon it appeared there might be some rain. Rain clouds built up over the mountains and maybe there would be some relief to the heat but only a few drops fell. The main storm never made it.

Sometime later the soldiers tried it again. But this time as the men drew sniper fire in the open a squad of NVA peppered the snipers with fire after seeing the snipers' muzzle flashes. They had to change their positions in a hurry, moving around to a different area in a fallen tree.

Now, the toll was telling on the two Marines. Both of them looked haggard and gaunt from the long on-going ordeal. But no matter how bad it was for the snipers it was easy for them to sympathize with the besieged NVA.

After dark on the fourth night of the siege the soldiers behind the dike swiftly retaliated with a volley of their own that again sent the snipers scurrying to avoid their fire. No longer were they safe shooting at night because the enemy quickly picked up their location from the flash of their firing.

Abruptly a slow rain set in and provided relief for both the besieged and the snipers who decided that they had enough. By the dawn of the fifth day they called in and requested artillery to give them some time to clear out before they rained down a barrage on the remainder of the company in the rice paddies.

To make sure these two got back without getting into any more trouble, a patrol was sent out to meet them. With this escorting patrol of excited Marines Hathcock and Burke made their way back to Hill 55. In the background they heard the distant thunder of artillery shells exploding on the remainder of the company hiding behind the dike.

If there were any survivors, and there were a small number of them captured later, none of them could believe that only two Marine snipers had been responsible for almost wiping out their entire NVA Company. Before he left the Marines, Carlos Hathcock had 93 confirmed kills and more than 200 unconfirmed. He became a U.S. Marine legend.

Sadly, not long after this mission Lance Corporal John

Roland Burke lost his life. What follows courtesy of Wikipedia are the details of his life, his Navy Citation and condolences from his friends.

John Roland Burke born February 6, 1944 in Clearwater, Florida.
Died June 6, 1967 (aged 23) in Quang Tri, South Vietnam
Allegiance: United States of America
Service/branch: United States Marine Corps
Years of service: 1965 - 1967
Rank: Corporal
Unit: 1st Battalion 26th Marines
Battles/wars: Vietnam War

Corporal John Roland Burke (February 6, 1944-June 6, 1967) was a sniper in the United States Marine Corps. For his accomplishments he was posthumously awarded the Navy Cross after he was killed in action at Khe Sanh.

Awards & decorations
Navy Cross citation
Bronze star
Navy Cross
Purple Heart National Defense Service Medal: Vietnam Service Medal w/ 1 service star
Military Merit Medal: Vietnam Gallantry Cross w/palm, Vietnam Campaign Medal.

Navy Cross citation
For extraordinary heroism while serving as a Sniper Team Leader with Headquarters and Service Company, First Battalion, 26th Marines, 3rd Marine Division (Reinforced), in the Republic of Vietnam on 6 June 1967. Assigned the mission of defending an outpost on Hill 950 at Khe Sanh, Quang Tri Province, Corporal Burke's team was taken under attack by a numerically superior enemy force. During the initial assault,

Corporal Burke was wounded by an enemy grenade. Ignoring his wound, he administered first aid to a severely wounded comrade and placed him in a relatively safe position, covering the wounded man with his own body to protect him from further injury. Heeding a call for help from outside the bunker, he unhesitatingly went to the aid of another Marine. While he and a companion were moving the man to the security of the bunker an enemy grenade exploded, knocking him and his comrade into the bunker. Although seriously wounded, he moved the wounded man to a tunnel to protect him from the devastating enemy fire. With all his team members casualties, Corporal Burke unhesitatingly and with complete disregard for his own safety armed himself with grenades, and shouting words of encouragement to his men, stormed from the bunker in a valiant one-man assault against the enemy positions. While firing his weapon and throwing grenades at the enemy positions, Corporal Burke was mortally wounded. By his dauntless courage, bold initiative and devotion to duty, he was instrumental in stopping the enemy attack and saving his men from possible further injury or death, thereby reflecting great credit upon himself and the United States Marine Corps and upholding the highest traditions of the United States Naval Service. He gallantly gave his life for his country. JOHN R. BURKE

We remember John Burke
Posted on 11/12/02 - by Al Galbraith
The Clearwater (FL) High School Class of 1962 held its 40th reunion this summer, and there was much discussion of John. We lost "only" one man in Viet Nam, but why did it have to be John -- a quiet young man, basketball player, good student, an all-around decent guy. Not the kind to go "gung ho," but not the kind to shrink from duty or fail to do what had to be done when the lives of his buddies were on the line. God bless you through all eternity, John. We miss you.

A Marine's Marine and Carlos Hathcock's best partner.
Posted on 9/29/01 - by David R. Sanchez

There can be no greater proof of John's worth than the loving words of Hathcock whose own life and record are legendary. *"All wars kill our bravest and strongest and the only compensation for John's death is not medals but the recounting of his life and actions to succeeding generations. How many of our bravest and worthiest proved their valor in the darkness and chaos of Vietnam and Korea and Europe with only God watching? The sadness is that both sides were brave and the politicians like McNamara and generals like Westmoreland used our best for their ambitions. History is written by the living whose memory can be selective and self-serving."*

In the Beginning....

Heroes come in every size, shape, and nationality, but one thing is often the same for all of them. Most come from a background of poverty and adversity. Things they fought hard to overcome. Perhaps this struggle to be better is what made them such strong characters determined to do what they did; to excel in extraordinary ways.

Carlos Norman Hathcock II was born to an impoverished couple in Little Rock, Arkansas on May 20, 1942. His father was a welder. When his dad came back from World War II he gave his 3-year-old son an inoperable German Mauser rifle he had bought as a war souvenir. When the boy was old enough and strong enough he carried that rifle into the woods with him and his dog where he fought imaginary battles with an imaginary enemy. When Carlos was 10-years-old he was given a Buck Jones Daisy pump BB-gun as a birthday present. Like almost every other American boy everywhere he became a good shot with this air rifle. Sadly, however, Carlos' BB-gun beginning had a bad ending.

Carlos saw a meal on the wing when he eyed the fat pigeons that flew around the gables of a nearby seminary. Stealthily the boy stalked the birds. He was just drawing a bead on one of them with his trusty BB-gun when a Sister came running out of the seminary in full black habit with sparks flying out of her eyes. She screamed, *"Stop that! Stop it right now!"*

Carlos froze in his tracks.

She stood over him glaring down at him and pointing a very long white accusatory finger at him.

"Young man," she said sharply with a quivery voice. "Don't you know that *Thou Shalt Not Kill?*"

"No'm," murmured Carlos, scared out of his wits.

"Give me that gun at once." She reached out, grabbed the barrel and jerked it away from him. The gun fired, the BB hit a mud-puddle and splashed muddy water on the nun's neat habit.

"See! See!" she shouted. "Tell your parents that if they want this gun back they will have to come and talk to me about it." The white-faced nun spun around on her heel and stalked quickly back to the seminary holding the object of her disapproval at arm's length in case it still might be dangerous.

Needless to say his parents never came and talked to the nun about the BB gun. Mainly because Carlos wisely forgot to tell them about the incident. How he explained the Daisy's sudden disappearance we will never know.

The big day came when his mother and grandmother gave him a Sears and Roebuck Higgins single shot bolt action .22 rifle for his birthday. Made by Marlin this popular rifle with its open sights was the least expensive of all the .22 rifles being offered then.

Carlos immediately took his brand new .22 rifle to the woods, sighted it in, [for non-shooters sighting or zeroing in a rifle means adjusting the gun's sight so the rifle bullet will hit what you aim at over a specific distance] and began hunting. He became a very good shot. Years later when someone asked him who taught him to shoot like that, he said, "I did. There was nobody to teach me so I had to learn myself." From then on he came home with an unending bag limit of squirrels and rabbits to help feed the family. By then his mother and hard-drinking father had divorced. Carlos was now being brought up by his mother and grandmother at his grandmother's where she lived in the country near Little Rock. Carlos was living the good life of an outdoor hunter spending as much of his time as possible in the woods. At the same time he was sharpening his skills with his rifle and learning how to take care of himself as a woodsman. He knew about the stealth and stillness needed when he was in game country. He once told an interviewer years later, "As a young'n, I'd go sit in the woods and wait a spell. I'd just wait for the rabbits and the squirrels, 'cause sooner or later a squirrel would be in that very tree, or a rabbit would be coming by that very log. I just knew it. Don't know why, just did."

He was a lean, trim, quiet-spoken youngster who never lost his country Arkansas accent. Carlos was eager to learn about the life of a woodsman because it meant that now for the first time he could contribute something worthwhile to the family's well-being. What he was learning in those formative years would save his life repeatedly during the Vietnam War years later. Both his mother and grandmother told him how much they appreciated him bringing home game for the family.

In one way or another, hunters all grew up sharing similar hunting experiences. Those who grew up on farms or lived in rural areas got introduced to it earlier than city kids. If your family members were not hunters or fishermen in the past, then chances were good that you might not be one either. But usually for those whose parents were outdoorsmen, so too were their kids.

Carlos Hathcock knew from his early years that he wanted to one day become a United States Marine. At one time a Marine lived downstairs from him and his family and he always admired the young man. He liked his sharp, colorful uniform and he liked his calm, cool bearing. This was the kind of man he wanted to be. Once Carlos made up his mind to do something, he seldom changed it. He once told an interviewer that there's no such thing as "can't." He said, "My Daddy told me a long time ago, when I was a little feller, he said, 'Son, there is no such word as 'can't'. Some things are a little harder to accomplish than others, but the word 'can't' does not stay in my vocabulary. Don't let it stay in yours.' And, since then, I've used the same thing. There's no such word as can't.'"

Carlos left high school in the 6th grade and never looked

back. At 15 he took a job working for a concrete construction company. From then on life taught him everything else he learned. He could hardly wait until he was old enough to join the U.S. Marines. He got his wish when he turned 17 in 1959. At that time he was 5 feet 10 inches tall, weighed 160-pounds and had handled so many heavy bags of cement that he could hoist anything his own weight over his head.

Three years later he married Josephine Winstead from North Carolina and she gave birth to their son, Carlos Hathcock III. In boot camp Carlos shot so well that he was rated an Expert. He entered and repeatedly won competitive shooting contests. He won many shooting championship awards in the service. Eventually, Cpl. Carlos N. Hathcock II was awarded the 1965 prestigious Wimbledon Cup, a trophy given to the winner of the 1000-yard shooting match.

When they shipped Carlos overseas to Vietnam as a member of the Military Police he soon tired of that and wanted some kind of duty that would get him into action. Overseas when the Marines realized that Carlos had a natural gift for shooting they moved him to Hill 55 where he trained as a sniper. It was the happiest he had ever been in the service. Suddenly he found himself enjoying every minute of being a Marine. He progressed in leaps and bounds under the tutelage of Lieutenant (later Major) E. J. Land.

Hill 55 (also known as Nui Dat Son or Camp Muir) was a hill 16km southwest of Da Nang, Quang Nam Province, Vietnam. The hill was located 3km northeast of the confluence of the Yen, Ai Nghia and La Tho rivers. During the first Indonesian War a battalion of French soldiers were wiped out there by the Viet Minh. The Viet Cong later mined it. And after the Marines moved in and de-mined it, the 1ˢᵗ Marine Division Sniper Platoon trained snipers there under Captain Land. Hill 55 was prized because it was high enough terrain to overlook the surrounding countryside of jungle, native villages, trails, and rice paddies collectively known by the Marines during the Vietnam War as Indian Country. This area was working alive with Viet Cong. Hathcock called these gooks, Hamburgers. It was here, at Hill 55 that Carlos Hathcock made what in 1967 was the longest confirmed sniper shot ever made. I have written about Carlos' Longest Mission in detail. I have tried to write about these following events as they actually occurred including important details. Following them are comments his comrades made who met Hathcock as he was fighting his last valiant battle with Multiple Sclerosis. Their personal observations were to me some of the most touching of all tributes paid to him.

5

The Longest Shot

Vietnam 1967

Hill 55 had sandbagged projections at different levels where snipers took turns scoping the surrounding country for possible enemy targets. Anyone carrying a weapon or transporting weapons was considered an enemy target. Some of the trails that could be seen were natural paths along which the enemy, more often at night, moved supplies to their forces. There were other times when these enemy couriers dressed the same as the local native farmers moved arms even during daylight hours unaware apparently that powerful binoculars and gun-scopes from on high were watching their every move.

It became apparent to Sergeant Hathcock and Captain Land that a lot more of this enemy activity was occurring within the range of their binoculars but far out of range of their rifles. The enemy knew they could get away with it because no rifle anyone had then could reach out and tap them that far away.

What they didn't know was that one sniper at least thought he knew how he might do it. The one weapon the Marines had that could indeed reach out that far was their M2 heavy machine gun. Carlos and his fellow marines set it up on one of the finger projections that looked out over the sprawling country below. It was no small feat positioning this weapon because the gun itself weighed 84-pounds and its assembled tripod added another 44-pounds. In WWI the Cavalry's packhorses handled that job but today those heavy machine guns are easiest fired in the field mounted on something mechanized. But in its Hill 55 configuration where it would remain in one place that was protected, Carlos figured it was the best long-range varmint weapon they had. It could reach out twice as far as his .30-06 Winchester. Once he fashioned a mount that would hold his long 8-power Unertl sniper riflescope on the top right hand side of the gun's receiver so he could zero in the weapon, he was in business. The maximum effective range of this machine gun was almost one and a half miles. Carlos zeroed it in flat so that his crosshairs on a target at 2500 yards would put the 700-grain two-and-one-half inch pointed lead projectile precisely where he aimed it.

Sitting cross-legged behind the gun with his hands on the two spade-shaped handles he could use the tripod's control knobs and traversing system to aim this weapon precisely. Between the machine gun's handgrips were the bolt release lever and the v-shaped butterfly trigger that you tripped by pressing with your thumb, or both thumbs. When the bolt release lever was locked up the gun fired automatically. When the bolt release lever was locked down, it fired single shots the way Carlos wanted it to fire.

This wasn't the first time the M2 was used in this manner. Thanks to the work of ordinance expert Bill Brophy, troops used the M2 for sniping during the Korean War. Brophy was the genius that first pioneered this. Hathcock now pioneered its use for the first time in extra-long-range sniping. Today, of course, many nations' arsenals include the .50 caliber rifle. But what made all the difference in Hathcock's 1966 configuration was that this heavy weapon removed the possibility that the shooter could screw up the shot by jerking. If his zeroing in was accurate the sniper now had a totally steady aiming platform. The weapon's 700-grain bullet struck its target with such explosive force that whoever took its impact on the receiving end never knew what hit them.

For the last couple days, Carlos and his spotter Staff

Sergeant Charlie Roberts using an M49 20-power spotting scope hunkered down in their sand-bagged finger letting their eyes roam over the endless miles of verdant green valley below with its numerous villages and it unending rice paddies. Wisps of smoke from the village cook fires mixing with the morning mists always created a blanketing fog that disappeared in the growing heat of the day. Jungle birds soared in and out of the canopied jungle, as the two Marines scanned the distant scene searching for things that looked out of place.

Nothing caught their attention until late afternoon when Roberts picked up a lone bicyclist pushing his overloaded bike up a hill toward a main path leading toward several villages. He looked like a young fellow but what caught the spotter's interest was how hard the courier worked to get up that grassy incline. What was so heavy that he carried?

As the biker came into view more broadside to the Marines they saw he had rifles looped by their shoulder straps hanging on his handlebars, and large haversacks on each side that bulged with what the snipers guessed could be curved banana clips of ammunition.

All the Vietnamese soldiers looked smaller and younger than they actually were. The Marines knew too that the Vietcong often threatened the local villagers into making their children carry supplies or even go to war against the Americans. Carlos had no stomach for taking out civilians forced to carry supplies for the Vietcong. So when the two of them were sure of what they were seeing, Roberts said, "Maybe a warning shot will change his mind and one of our patrols can pick up his load"

"Just what I was thinking," said Carlos. "He can't carry that stuff if he has no bike."

Carlos turned a knob and moved the cross hairs of his scope low to the ground and some distance ahead as the courier climbed on his bike and began pedaling into the sniper's line of fire. Carlos' target was at 2,500 yards, right where he had zeroed in the M2.

At just the right moment the .50 caliber heavy machine gun went *ka-pow* coughing out its single projectile and the front wheel of the bicycle disappeared. The courier flew head over heels over his handlebars. When he bounced back up on his feet, there was no doubt that he was angry. He looked up toward the Hill, reached down, grabbed a rifle, shoved in a banana clip of ammo and as he brought it up to his shoulder to fire, Carlos thumbed off another round. The shooter was blown backward halfway down the hill he had just climbed.

No one came to claim his body until just before sundown when several villagers with a litter came and got him. No one touched the broken bike or the rifles that were picked up by a returning patrol of Marines, along with the bags of ammo.

"Those weapons and cartridges won't ever be turned against any Marine in this war," thought Carlos as he and Roberts shut down their operation for the day and headed for their hooches.

"Seeya in the morning," said Roberts.

"You bet," said Carlos.

At first light both Marines were back at their post, uncovering the M2 and getting ready for another day of surveillance. This one might prove more interesting since a battalion of Marines planned to make a sweep through the areas below and the snipers had an idea that there might be some VC sneaking out around the edges trying to evade confrontation. At least they could hope.

The troops were choppered in and the sweep took place. Everyone on the Hill heard the action and followed its progress by the sounds of the gunfire. In the course of the morning Hathcock and Roberts were joined by a Major who enjoyed being in this lofty place where his binoculars and his radioman filled him in on what was happening below. Whenever one or more VC slipped past the flankers and broke out of the cover to try for the distant safety of the mountains, the spotters would see them and Hathcock took them out.

The sweep turned out to be a large success with a great many of the VC wiped out. By late afternoon things had calmed down. The major retired to document what he had seen of the sweep and a lieutenant who had been in the action that morning joined Hathcock and Roberts in their sniping finger.

Soon Hathcock called the lieutenant's attention to a guerilla he spotted who stepped out of the jungle and started along the berm of a distant rice paddy.

The lieutenant found him with his binoculars. "Whoa, that guy's way out of range, isn't he? He's stopping and looking around. Hey, I think that's a Chinese rifle he's carrying! Can you get him from here?"

"Yessir," said Hathcock who had already put the black crosshairs of his scope on the man's chest. He's at 2,500-yards. Right where I zeroed it. You're right about the rifle. It's a Chinese K-44 slung across his back. "

"Then take him out," ordered the lieutenant.

What neither Hathcock nor the lieutenant expected suddenly happened. Just when Hathcock's thumb pushed down on the butterfly trigger the target bent down toward the water.

As the man straightened up the high-speed missile caught him right under his chin.

That was the longest confirmed kill he ever made. In fact, in 1967 Vietnam Carlos N. Hathcock II set the record for the longest confirmed kill at 2,250 meters (2,460 yds), a record, which stood for 35 years until 2002, when it was broken in Afghanistan by Canadian Forces sniper, Arron Perry.

6

The Apache

Vietnam 1966

High above the valley of rice paddies and jungle on Hill 55, nothing got one's attention faster than a sudden scream in the night. It always came as a shock. *Whap!* Like a bolt of lightning. It stabbed into the hearts of the men trying to sleep in the sniper camp's sandbagged bunkers.

At first, it created confusion. What in God's name was *that*? Men sat up and strained to hear. All they heard was silence. That wasn't the night jungle in the valley below them. Then suddenly came another high-pitched scream of the most awful kind. The scream of a man's tormented soul. Sweat beads popped out on their foreheads. Chills ran down their sweaty backs making their skin crawl as though a roach had run over them. Hands reached to grip weapons. They gritted their teeth at the sound and helplessly clenched their fists.

The sound of a man screaming traveled far in the silent hot jungle night. They knew their night's sleep was over now. The living nightmare of the Apache lady's terrible torture of some helpless soul was just beginning. Most of them had heard about the stripped corpses, bright red in the sun. They knew what was happening…the slow, torturous skinning of a human being that would go on and on with his screams all night long.

Those who had heard it before cursed and stuffed whatever was at hand into their ears to try and shut it out. But it never helped. The men's minds were too focused on the horror of what was happening to one of their own, the living hell the Apache made for everyone within hearing. She knew what it did to the troops. It tore them up. It made their very souls cringe. It deprived them of sleep. It made numb robots of them the next day, robots that made the soldiers more vulnerable than ever to attack. Someone needed to do something about her but nobody knew how to do it.

They had tried, but always failed. She traveled light with a squad of bodyguard goons that surrounded her with armed defenses including captured Claymore mines and numerous trip-wired traps. Long after the fact when they found the clearings where she operated along the valley's meandering jungle-choked river, all she left for them was the bloody skinned remains of her victim tied spread-eagled on a bamboo frame with his genitals jammed down his throat. Only the un-skinned battered head resembled anything human.

"Who the hell is this bitch anyway?" new recruits always asked.

Scuttlebutt said she was an attractive woman in her late thirties who had a sadistic hatred for all foreigners in this war. All she thought about was how to torture all soldiers. In one instance she had her cohorts starve several huge rats. She cut a hole in the bottom of a woven basket and shoved it down over the head of a captured soldier bound to a rack. Then she dumped in the starving rats and sewed the top shut. Those who recovered the man's remains the next day said there was nothing left of the head but some hair and a fleshless, gnawed skull.

She enjoyed taking her hatred out on the foreign soldiers she captured alive. After a night with the Apache the sleepless troops expected an attack the next night. Sometimes it came, sometimes it didn't. The tension of waiting for an attack that didn't come was also part of her torture. But when it came it was a dozy.

It often started with a signal of some kind, a rocket, a whistle or a lone bugle call from the enemy. Everyone on the hill knew what that meant. They grabbed their weapons and raced to their positions. The machine gunners readied themselves. Flares lit up the night in a flickering rosy glare. The black edges of the jungle worked alive with movement as though someone had kicked open a giant bed of fireants.

First came a barrage of mortar fire. The Marines could hear the mortars being tubed. This shelling was designed to drive the defenders into cover while the sappers came in. Along the perimeter they came with mats and brush, anything to cover the coils of razor wire. This allowed other sappers with rocket-propelled Chincon grenades, and satchel charges to crawl up the hill under the wire extending homemade Bangalore torpedoes — half pound TNT blocks between bamboo poles to blow the wire and open a way through the perimeter defenses for the troops to follow.

But the Marines were ready for them and the night lit up with tracer bullets as they mowed them down as fast as they came. Still, wave after wave of yelling black-clad soldiers poured in through the breach firing as they struggled up through the bloody mass of mangled bodies and razor-bladed wire, climbing over the bodies of the men before them. The sounds of screaming were drowned out by the mechanical rapidfire chatter of the heavy machine guns coupled with the sharp cracks of rifle fire and sudden grenade explosions. The air filled with fire and smoke, a living over-heated hell that went on far too long. Then again a rocket was fired or a bugle sounded and the charge was aborted because the Marines had not taken cover but stayed to fight off the charge with a hail of hot lead. After that signal the noise dropped off; the firing diminished. The black-clad figures fell back and faded into the jungle leaving behind a bloody mess with the smell of death and brimstone over it.

Sergeant Carlos Hathcock knew that something had to be done to take out the Apache but he couldn't figure how to do it. The woman and her goons were slick as snot. They came and went freely in Indian Country under the close protection of the Vietcong. The psychological damage she was doing to our troops was considerable.

Daily Carlos was going out on missions almost without end. He would come back from one mission, restock his ammo, grab another handful of snacks and C-Rats and head out again, to be gone for days making kills that were never reported because there was no one to confirm what he did. Made no difference to him. He didn't like the idea of snipers competing for kills anyway. He felt that every one of the enemy he could take out meant that one or more Marines would live. That was the most important thing to him. He felt that anyone who kept a scorecard of kills so they competed with some other sniper was disrespectful of what they were there to do.

He later said that he gradually got use to it, knowing that he was accomplishing his goal. He preferred doing his missions by himself because he never wanted to be responsible for someone else's life that perhaps lacked some of the woodsman's skills that kept Carlos alive. In fact after his service he was proud to be able to say that he never lost a man while he was on a sniper mission.

Gradually of course he partnered with spotters whom he admired and respected as being equal to hisself in these skills. Two he always admired in this category and who usually accompanied him as his spotter were his one-time commanding officer, Captain E. J. Land, and Lance Corporal Johnnie Burke. What deadly teammates these guys made!

But soon there came one too many victims from the Apache that got Hathcock's instant attention. She had recently caught a fresh young Marine private and tortured him within earshot of Hill 55 all night long and into the next day. No one knows what she said to him or exactly what the sequence was of his tortures because none of her victims ever lived long enough to describe them. So what follows is a rough idea of how it might have happened based on the injuries sustained by this young Marine private who ended up taking his last tortured breath in front of Carlos Hathcock. Here's how it might have occurred:

The scene is a jungle clearing with a huge fire burning in its center. To one side is a vertical bamboo rack with the naked marine spread-eagled on it. During the day the Apache wore a wide brim conical hat like the villagers. But now her long black hair flowed around her beautiful Asiatic face as she came into the firelight. Her burly armed companions stood in the shadows watching the scene. They had ringed the jungle well away from the clearing with the Marines' own captured Claymore mines. Tied to trees facing away from the clearing each was rigged with hidden trip wires. If any soldiers from the hill were foolish enough to try to come to the Marine's rescue, they would get the full blast of hundreds of steel balls for their trouble.

Dressed in the loose-fitting black silk shirt and pants the VC wore she danced before the man tied spread-eagled on the vertical bamboo frame. The upright frame gave her access to either side of his taunt body. The scene flickered with moving shadows from the flames that licked the night. In the jungle background moonlight glittered on a narrow river flowing beside the camp.

The Apache danced around her prisoner brandishing a long curved slender-bladed knife that she always held high overhead making sure that it was seen constantly by the doomed man on the bamboo frame. Over and over she held it before his eyes talking to him as she showed off the weapon that would soon cut him to ribbons. She did it with each of her victims.

"Hello young Marine," she whispered seductively. "Welcome to our little party. How you like being main attraction? You like? You like me? Oh yes. I like you too."

She twirled around him. The man rigid with fear stared wide-eyed at her. Mainly because that afternoon while her goons held him down she methodically sliced off his eyelids. The soldiers on the Hill heard his screams and knew what they were in for the next few hours.

"I no want you to miss the show," she smiled at him. As a boy a scene of horror flashed through his mind as he remembered reading Christopher Wren's books about the French Foreign Legion and how the desert Tauregs tortured captives by burying them in ant hills, cutting off their eyelids and pouring honey over their heads. He screamed even louder at that thought.

During the next few hours he fainted repeatedly from the pain. Whenever he did her goons sloshed him down with a bucket of river water to bring him back to realty. The Apache was in no hurry. Systematically she broke each of his fingers; then she began slicing off his skin. The only miraculous thing was that he lived through it all. Obviously the Apache didn't want the young marine to die. She had one more special treat for him.

It came at dawn when she cut his bindings and he slid off the rack. It was just his upper body that was totally raw; she had purposely done nothing to his legs so that he could still stand.

She prodded him along a trail leading to the edge of the jungle. A short ways further was the gradual incline up to Hill 55 and the heavy coils of razor wire.

She smiled at the boy. "I let you go now Marine. You no good to me no more. Maybe you friends shoot you before you get to them." She stood in front of him. She said, "I give you one more souvenir to remember me by. With one swift sweep of her sharp knife she emasculated him.

His piercing scream brought sleepless Marines tumbling out of their hooches

She hissed, "Run…run…Marine!"

Gushing blood he staggered toward the wire shouting unintelligibly; waving his bloody arms to prevent the guards shooting him.

Hathcock was at the wire when the boy fell in front of him.

Despite helping arms of everyone, there was nothing

anyone could do to save him.

Tears ran down Carlos's cheeks and under his breath he swore to this tortured young Marine, that the Apache witch would pay for this horror if it was the last thing he ever did.

On all the missions he went on for the next few weeks, Carlos hoped to run into the VC sniper group of goons that she seemed to control. It was a month later when another detachment reported spending a sleepless night listening to another one of her torture sessions.

As soon as they heard about it Hathcock and Land took off in that direction to try and intercept the group near a shallow river crossing commonly used by the VC on their forays in and out of Indian Country.

The two lay in ambush all day long with no luck. As they were running out of daylight Land was urging Hathcock to give it up so they could get back to camp.

Hathcock stubbornly refused to go, saying he had a gut feeling that they were going to see action soon. The two were almost in an argument over it when a group of five VC stealthily appeared across the river.

Hathcock was not sure this was the Apache and her goons since they all dressed alike with the same wide-brimmed cone hats and black pajamas. They crossed the river and started toward the snipers' hide when one of them stepped aside and squatted to relieve herself.

There was no longer any question in their minds. As the woman stood up and started toward the snipers with her long sniper rifle slung across her back, the others called to her to go in another direction. But for some reason she kept coming on.

Hathcock put the Winchester's crosshairs on her chest and fired. She dropped and didn't move. For good measure he put another one into her and under his breath he told her who those two shots were for.

The Apache was never heard from again.

7

Carlos Hathcock's Longest Mission

Vietnam 1966

As the black cross against the indigo blue sky rose leisurely on the large upwelling warm air current the raptor's wings were set so rigidly he looked like a small fixed wing model airplane from below but from above the black-winged kite's eyes missed nothing. Or so it thought.

With the raptor's astonishingly sharp eyesight capable of zooming in on the slightest movement in the green and sun-dried yellow grassy plain below, it scanned for prey. It saw the large white manmade structure in the midst of the grassy plain and it saw the men in twos plodding slowly around the vast grassy plain. Around the structure were many other small man-structures. Too much commotion for there to be any prey thought the raptor as he wheeled off to look more closely at the openings through the overhead canopy of the nearby dense green jungle.

What his raptor sharp eyes failed to see far below in the yellowish-green foot-tall grass was a blob of green and yellow vegetation that moved through the surrounding grass with the speed of an earthworm. From above the raptor might have seen the narrow compressed nature of the grass trail that followed behind the barely moving shape but the kite would have thought nothing of it because the other man-shapes had left hundreds of interconnecting similar trails behind them as they moved in a general circular pattern around the large white structure. Scattered around the field close to the house were also several heavy machinegun emplacements seldom used but always manned in case of an aerial attack. But since this was a peaceful country it was unlikely.

What the kite failed to see was sniper Carlos Hathcock II who the night before had changed all the natural ferns and grasses that sprouted lavishly from all of the parallel slits in his camouflaged utilities. The new ones more closely matched the sun-scorched grasses of this long green emptiness that lay ahead of him. Across this wide-open area the gentle warm breeze moved the deep grass like a slowly undulating green sea. With his rifle clutched to his chest the sniper blended in perfectly as he crawled slowly on his side to minimize the trail he made through the grass. His grease-painted face matched the slightly greenish-yellow grass and his slow-motion forward movements were so controlled and intentional that after crawling all night and part of a day he already ached from this forced slow movement. In fact every muscle of his body screamed for him to jump up and stretch. But Carlos had mastered the art of this slothful movement and from long practice it made him push the pain of this inconvenience into the background of his mind.

Normally Carlos kept his cheek to the ground as he followed his compass course. He knew exactly where he wanted to go and how long it would take him to get there. Under his wide brimmed camouflaged bush hat whose band for once did not sport his trademark white feather he carried nothing that might identify him on this particular mission. He kept his nearly closed slit eyes averted because he had no need to look up.

Whenever he did the sniper never focused on what was close to him. He never saw the grass, he saw through it. Though he had been bitten repeatedly by insects he crawled over, he treated the pain the same way he did his aching cramped body. He forced all those pains into the back of his mind, telling himself repeatedly that they would stop hurting if he thought hard enough that they were numb, and by golly it sometimes worked! Carlos had found he could control the discomfort and live with it. There was no other way.

All of his other senses he treated just the opposite. He turned them on high alert. He strained to listen to every sound. The swishing of grass could warn of something approaching. If he disturbed a nesting bird its sudden flight and annoyed cry might tell an alert sentry that something had disturbed that bird and it might be an enemy. Hathcock's sense of smell was equally fine-tuned. He smelled the enemy's cooking fires at a certain time and occasionally he smelled the sweet aroma of the sentries smoking pot. If he smelled a fishy odor he knew they were very close to him because they all reeked of the stinking dried fish that was their common diet along with a fist-sized ball of sticky rice. He smelled the grasses and the fresh earth smells. He prayed not to crawl into an anthill and prayed to God not to let him crawl onto a deadly bamboo viper. Please God no poisonous snakes at all. And if you could please let it rain on me I would be more than happy for your kindness. Rain sent sentries into cover and he could move faster because it covered the sounds of his movements.

He had sipped canteen capfuls of water most of the evening before in preparation for what he figured would be at least three days and two nights of crawling. Before he left Hill 55 he ate the last meal he would eat for 72 hours. Before he started his crawl he did whatever business he had to do. No sniper ever wanted to be caught on his belly having to do Number Two. Since snipers on a mission existed on virtually no food but snacks, they managed to largely avoid having to do a Two for several days. But if he did have to go he knew he would just do it. When and if he had to do Number One there was no question about where either. He enjoyed its pleasant warmth. After days in country, men lost their human smell and smelled more like the scruffy unwashed animal they were. Just the way a sniper liked it. No perfumed aftershave or whiff of manly Irish Spring was going to cost him his life. No sir. But some snipers did sometimes add a mild insecticide to their grease paint. When an enemy with his twitchy finger on the trigger of his AK-47 is standing above you waiting for the slightest tell-tale movement it's hell not being able to flinch when a red ant walks boldly across your face and just for the hell of it takes a bite out of your nostril. So it never hurt to have a few drops of odorless anti-bug juice mixed in with your makeup. Of course it fit right in with the sweat, dirt and grime, charcoal smudges and other stuff that got mixed in with that greasy face paint. Sometimes you felt if there was a way to blank out the whites of your eyes by golly you'd do that too. Eyelid makeup worked for that. If there was any question of detection you just closed your eyes and prayed.

Whenever the pain of the stings and the cramps got almost more than he could bear Carlos managed to take the edge off his discomfort by thinking about happier times, especially the better times he had growing up. He recalled how eager he was to get old enough that his Mom and Dad would let him have a BB gun. Santa Clause brought it to him one Christmas. It was an authentic long dark brown stained wooden stock Buck Jones Daisy pump action air rifle and from that minute on every bird in his area of rural Arkansas learned to beware of the skinny little kid with the long BB gun. When his father came home from World War II with an inoperable German Mauser rifle he had bought, he gave it to his small son. When the boy was big enough to carry it Carlos took it to the woods where he had imagined shoot-outs with German and Japanese enemies.

Those were wonderful times for the always-poor family. But too often his parents argued fiercely. His father was a railroad worker in North Little Rock and then became a welder in Memphis, Tennessee. His father drank and that caused a lot of trouble. When his mother and father finally separated Carlos went to live with his grandmother. The boy always deeply appreciated the family spending their few dollars they could afford for his cherished things, especially when he was given his first real rifle, a J.C. Higgins .22 caliber single shot. From that day on he and his dog spent as much time as they could hunting together and bringing home squirrels, rabbits and occasionally pigeons, all game that he was proud to be able to provide for them on his own. Carlos remembered what care he took in zeroing in his first real rifle. He practiced and practiced shooting until it became second nature to him. He could hit anything he aimed at.

"As a young'n, I'd go sit in the woods and wait a spell," Hathcock once told an interviewer. "I'd just wait for the rabbits and the squirrels, 'cause sooner or later a squirrel would be in that very tree, or a rabbit would be coming by that very log. I just knew it. Don't know why, just did."

He left high school at 15 to take a job working for a concrete construction company. Even as a youngster he yearned to grow up to be a member of the U.S. Marine Corps. He saw a Marine who once lived downstairs from him. Carlos admired his colorful uniform and he liked how everyone treated the soldier with respect. The boy wanted that. He got his wish when he turned 17 in 1959. Three years later he married Josephine Winstead from North Carolina and she gave birth to their son, Carlos Hathcock III. When the Marines realized that Carlos had a natural gift for shooting they trained him as a sniper. He won many shooting championship awards in the service. Cpl. Carlos Hathcock was awarded the 1965 Wimbledon Cup, a trophy given to the winner of the 1000-yard shooting match.

Those were happy times and despite his concentration on where he was and what he was doing squirming along on his side in the field, those memories helped keep his mind off the pain of his extremely slow progress. Slow as he was he knew it was leading him into more dangerous territory. The odds of him being discovered were increasing as the rapidly growing heat of the day seemed determined to stew him in his own juices.

This mission had been something dreamed up by the powers that be in Intelligence. The CIA was into everything in

Vietnam. No one ordered Carlos to take on this mission. They said no one else could do it but him. Just when he was looking forward to going home at the end of his hitch, this came along. No one would tell him anything about it. Where it was and who he was to take out, was all Top Secret. At least at first. The brass made sure he understood that there was a good chance that whoever took it on might not return from it. And as far as they were concerned, he, Carlos, was probably the only one of their top snipers who could possibly carry it off. Even then the odds were against him pulling it off and coming out alive.

Think it over, they said. He did and he decided he'd rather not go. But they told him no one else could do it. He was their best chance. He had to decide whether to take it on without knowing anything about what he was getting into. All they told him was that it was a major operation of such importance that everything about it had to be hush, hush. Yeah, He had heard that song before. All they told him was that if it worked it could change the balance of the war.

Carlos figured if they felt that other snipers would lose their lives trying to pull it off, he decided what the hell he might as well take it on and do the best he could.

Once he gave them his decision, they supplied him with maps, aerial photos and details of this very special target. In the end he wasn't even sure if he was going into North Vietnam, Cambodia or Laos. But the target was an important North Vietnam Army general. He studied the photograph of the portly man in full uniform regalia. He looked to be in his fifties. Intel apparently felt that this individual's command was a major log-jam to their battle plans. Supposedly by taking him out, things would vastly improve for our forces. Unless the target was Ho himself, Carlos largely doubted that.

He studied the material they gave him. Especially the aerial photos showing the wide-open country he had to cross to get within range of his target. It was a huge grassy meadow watched day and night by roving NVA guard patrols. His all night crawl to take out the Frenchman was nothing compared to this. He roughly calculated it would take him at least three days to worm his way to about 700 yards from the French Colonial house that served as the general's field headquarters. It stood in the middle of the meadow with his troops bivouacked around it. He would be unable to get any closer than that. There would only be time for one shot, one kill… one he had to make absolutely accurate. In other words he had to hit the center of a 2-foot-square target at the end of *seven* football fields lined up one after another!

With a magnifying glass he studied the terrain photos and saw the shadow of a slight gully depression that ran parallel to the course he hoped to crawl. It led straight back to the cover of the jungle. A possible escape route if he managed to get that far before sentries cut him down.

One thing about this mission if he pulled it off, he would need air support in a hurry. Killing the general would be like kicking a beehive. Those killer bees would instantly swarm after the kicker. Crack NVA trackers would be on his trail in no time. They would radio ahead for patrols to cut him off. This point needed resolving right away because he sure didn't intend to stick around for those hamburgers to catch him. Passing on his concerns to his handlers they soon came up with a plan. When Intel reported that the general was now in residence everyone decided that it was time to go.

As usual Carlos would travel light. This time lighter than he ever had before. Along with his compass, map and makeup, he took his k-bar knife, some ammo to feed his trusty glass-bedded Winchester Model 70 .30-06 with its long Unertl 8-power scope, and nothing else!

The squad that would accompany him to his departure point awaited him at the Landing Zone. With everyone aboard the chopper set off flying straight toward the slowly setting sun. It was not a long flight. Once they all dropped off and moved silently through the jungle the group of men expertly accompanied him to their final goal and just as swiftly without him they faded back into the jungle for their pickup.

The timing was perfect. As the sun dropped below the distant horizon Carlos stood at the edge of the tree-line looking out across the vast meadow that spread out before him. That sea of green was to be his stalking ground where he would move totally unseen slower than a sloth for the next three days and two nights.

He prepared himself by spending a couple hours replacing the camouflaging vegetation he wore threaded through the slots of his utilities. During that time he hydrated himself thoroughly with sips from his canteen. Then with a canopy of twinkling stars overhead, he went supine, turned on his side and clutching his rifle to him he crawled out into the night and into the grass that stood 12 inches above his head.

It had taken him hours to get to where he was but some 30 paces from where he began, he heard the swishing of grass; the low sound of voices as two NVA sentries slowly approached him.

He froze, hugging the ground. His heart pounding as rivulets of sweat streamed down his face.

The guards came so close to him that one almost stepped on him. But they were not expecting any enemy attack so they were not too alert. Carlos could tell by the soft murmur of their voices that they were just putting in their time, enjoying the cooler temperatures of the evening air. Eventually they moved on until the sound of their passing faded from his hearing. He stayed where he was without moving a muscle for another ten minutes then he began his worm crawl once again.

He had long ago checked his course direction with his small compass, noting that it matched that of a celestial constellation so that was the direction he crawled through the night.

Whether or not he slept at all was something he really never remembered. He had long ago mastered the ability to grab a few minutes catnap whenever he needed it. He never remembered it being voluntary, just that when he shortly came out of it he felt refreshed and continued his rhythmic crawl.

The first and second days passed that way, with only an occasional slow motion unscrewing of his canteen cap to take a small sip of water to assuage the terrible dryness of his mouth and the hunger that continually gnawed at him now.

As the third day passed into night he knew he was closing in on the slightly raised area he had seen in the aerial photographs where he figured it was going to be his best bet. He had wormed his way across almost 1200 yards of field. He had stopped that day to watch. Through his riflescope he saw the general leave by car, and return just before sunset.

He smelled the smoke of their cook fires that evening and the next morning. Knowing they were eating made his hunger all the more agonizing. What he had just gone through to get where he was seemed like an unending dream. All that kept him constantly alert now was the terrible aches and pains and the hunger that he could no longer numb out of his head. Worse, by now he carried an army of ants in his clothes. These large red devils delighted in occasionally biting him while feasting on his grimy body's salty sweat that now saturated him. He no longer smelled human. More like a caged animal that had urinated on itself. Since he had no food and only tiny sips of water there was little to eliminate.

As Carlos wormed toward his final destination what he feared came true and his blood froze in fear. Directly in front of him in the grass lay one of those fat green shoelace-sized bamboo snakes, staring at him with beady eyes and a flicking black forked tongue.

Carlos never moved. As he and the deadly viper stared at each other eye-to-eye he tried to control his hammering heart but it was useless. It thundered so hard he wondered in his mild delirium if the snake heard it…also he worried that the sweat dripping off his grease-painted face might actually trigger a strike. What if it hit him straight in the face! *Oh please God, not now!*

When the viper realized the man-thing in front of him made no threatening moves, he took that opportunity to slide himself off into the greenery and leave while the leaving was good.

Carlos breathed a long held sigh of relief. After giving the snake plenty of time to make good his escape, he began moving painfully again, feeling the large broken blisters on his shoulder, elbow and hip burning painfully once more as he resumed the heavy irritating dragging of his body along the rough ground that caused the weeping abrasion wounds in the first place.

Finally Carlos reached the slight rise. He rolled over and brought his rifle up into position. He took a long look at the front veranda of the large white sprawling colonial house before him. It appeared so close through his riflescope but he knew it in reality was a long way off. He knew because of the shimmering mirage he saw with his naked eye. And the slight effect the morning breeze had at that distance on the smoke from the cooking fires.

Methodically he began zeroing his rifle in on that front porch seven football fields away from him. He had done this kind of thing so much he did it automatically. He was creating the bubble of intensity he knew had to be around his every move and every calculation, every minute observation now.

To the right and left of his flanks he was well aware that there were installations of twin .51 caliber heavy machineguns that could mow him down and spit him out in pieces if they ever suspected who and where he was. But none of them ever expected a ground attack. That was too far from their wildest imaginations. They were focused on any possible air attack so Carlos and his bubble of intensity felt completely safe.

Carlos spread a camouflaged cloth on the ground under his rifle muzzle so that when he fired the gases would not blow up any dust that might give his hide away. The surrounding deep grass would hide his muzzle flash

As daylight came on with more intensity Carlos re-checked conditions and made the necessary calculations that would adjust his scope for a cross-hair dead center hit.

Then he assumed the prone firing position that always felt so familiar to him, the wide shoulder strap of his rifle pressing taunt and snugly comfortable against his left arm as he steadied everything, his breathing slow and easy.

Abruptly, the door on the veranda of the white house opened and an aide stepped out holding the door open followed briefly by the general in full uniform. His car had arrived minutes earlier and was awaiting him below the veranda steps as another aide stood holding open the rear passenger door.

As Carlos drew a bead on the man's full chest, the image suddenly blurred as the aide stepped in front of him to get to the general's left side as though intending to help him down the steps. At that moment the general stopped, put on his hat and looked out across the grass prairie at the fresh green colors of the new day.

At that instant with his sweaty cheek tight against the semi-Monte Carlo hump on the finely crafted Walnut stock of his Winchester Carlos exhaled and took a short breath, calmed himself and tightened his finger on the curved steel trigger.

In his concentration he hardly felt the rifle kick his shoulder or heard its sudden crack. His full concentration was now on the recoil stabilizing after-shock scope picture. The shot caught the general in the chest and blew him backward onto the porch.

Carlos didn't wait to see anything more. He crawled swiftly to the gully to his right, then tried to stand up and almost couldn't make it he was so cramped from three days crawling, but he did manage to stumble into the gully where he low-ran like a startled but wounded buck for the distant tree line.

Thankfully, he realized that in the sudden commotion everyone ran off in different directions believing perhaps that a ground attack was immediately in-coming.

By then Carlos had reached the cover of the jungle where he stayed low and kept to the heavy covering vegetation as best he could. As quickly as possible he reached his rendezvous point where a chopper and another protective squad of Marines quickly picked him up. A short time later he was wildly welcomed back at Hill 55 by a bunch of cheering comrades. Carlos grinned and waved in acknowledgement but he didn't take time to talk. His primary target now was to hit the Mess Hall as fast as he could.

Despite all the praise he received, Carlos later said he really saw no noticeable change to the balance of the war that the high brass figured would come due to the general's demise. All Carlos noticed was a marked increase in attacks from the North Vietnamese Army. Shortly afterward he was on his way home for a much anticipated leave to be with his wife and young son Carlos Hathcock III who was destined to make his own valorous career as had his Dad in the U.S. Marine Corps. The Marines never forgot what a magnificent mission Carlos performed for them in those four incredible days in 1966 Vietnam. He was and always will be an authentic modern American hero.

****

HOW CARLOS HATHCOCK ZEROED IN A RIFLE

(This condensation of an account by retired Marine Gus Fisher describes Gunny Sergeant Carlos Hathcock's training method for sighting in a sniper's rifle.)

Gus Fisher was a young Marine Sergeant when he came up to the Marine Corps Rifle Team as the junior Armorer. Growing up he had used shotguns to hunt small game and used a Model 74 Winchester .22 to learn basic marksmanship. In Marine boot camp he first learned about high-powered rifles and long-range shooting. During qualification trials he shot 7 consecutive bullseyes shooting offhand position at 200 yards. A crosswind messed up his accuracy after that so he ended up qualifying as a Sharpshooter.

While Fisher was going through the Armorer's program at Camp Pendleton, he bought a sporterized .308 German Mauser with a scope from a fellow Marine. "This I used for ground squirrel hunting," said Fisher, "but I was never satisfied with my zero on the rifle." A friend suggested he ask Gunny Sergeant Carlos Hathcock for help. Fisher didn't know about Hathcock's record but after the friend set up a meeting with him, Carlos told Fisher to thoroughly clean the bore and chamber of his rifle with patches, then meet him at noon at the 200 yard range with his hunting rifle and sling.

At the range Hathcock told Fisher to get down into his best prone position. He made a minor correction. Then Hathcock told him, "Before you shoot, the MOST important thing I want you to do is take your time and make it the best shot possible. It doesn't matter how long you take, just make it a good shot. ALSO, and this is as important, make sure you give me an accurate call on where you think the bullet hit the target."

Fisher made the shot and told Hathcock where he thought he hit.

Hathcock checked it with a spotting scope, grinned and said, "Not a bad call."

He then took a small screwdriver and made a slight adjustment to Fisher's scope. After that he had the Marine record every single bit of information in his log book about what the weather was like, the humidity, the temperature, how much wind and its direction, how he felt when the shot was fired; what ammo he used.

"I never imagined all the information he wanted," said Fisher. "He told me that even if a fly flew past and farted when I fired he wanted that info in my log book too." Then he told Fisher to thoroughly clean the bore and chamber and to have it dry when Fisher showed up at the range the next day at noon. Fisher said he was surprised that Hathcock only wanted him to fire one shot but since the lessons were free he wouldn't question his judgment.

"The next day, he told me the same thing. I called the shot and it was closer to the center of the bullseye. He made another slight adjustment and told me to clean the bore and chamber, dry the bore thoroughly and to come back the next day at noon. Then we recorded everything possible about that day. The following day, the shot was darn near exactly centered on the bullseye. Then he told me to clean and dry the bore before coming back the next day. Then we recorded everything about that day."

A week later Fisher's friend asked how he was doing. Fisher said he was doing well but wondered why Hathcock wanted him to fire only one round a day. The friend grinned and said, "How many shots do you need at a buck?"

For the first time Fisher realized that was the truth. All you really needed was one true shot. Fisher said that as the lessons with Hathcock continued that the master shooter continued this same process through the sitting position at 200 yards, then prone and sitting at 300 yards and 400 yards. Then he went down to 100 yards and offhand shooting as well. Daily Fisher recorded each shot and all the weather conditions in careful detail. Hathcock also had him mark his scope adjustment settings with a different color nail polish for each yard line.

After a few weeks when that was over, Fisher thought he had it all down and learned, and his scope was properly zeroed in. But no, Hathcock wasn't through with him yet.

"Carlos started calling me up on mornings it was foggy,

rainy, windy, high or low humidity, etc., etc. and we fired a single shot and recorded the sight settings and everything else about the day. (I actually used four or five log books by the time we were through and put that info all into one ring binder.) I almost had an encyclopedia on that rifle. (Grin.)"

After the next few months Fisher realized he had fired a single shot in virtually every kind of weather there was. Then, that next December hit them really cold. It felt like an Artic wind was blowing and there were four inches of snow covering everything and a freezing rain was falling when Hathcock phoned him to meet him at noon at the range.

Fisher knew him well enough by now to joke with him and he said, "Do you really want to watch me shoot in this kind of weather?" Hathcock chuckled and said, "Well, are you ever going to hunt in this kind of weather?" I sighed and said, "See you at noon."

By the following spring, Fisher had records for sight settings for the first shot out of a "cold" barrel for almost any weather, position and range he would use and every temperature, wind, humidity condition imaginable. Hathcock had told Fisher months before that was basically how he wanted all Marine snipers to sight in their rifles as only the first shot counts, though of course they would do it out to 700 yards on a walking target and further on a stationary target. They also practiced follow-up shots. For Marine Gus Fisher, he realized that he had been trained by the best. And as he said, "It gave me great confidence that I could dial in my scope for anything I would come across."

It was this kind of attention to detail that made Carlos Hathcock the outstanding expert sniper that he was. Those Marines he trained ended up equally the experts they all became. And since Carlos' methods are now part of the Marine training program, this too was part of his legacy to all Marines, his comrades in arms, this desire for them to always be the best of the best.

8

OF HEROES AND TRIBUTES

Vietnam 1969 and to the End

Back in Nam on his second tour Sergeant Carlos Hathcock and a group of other Marines were about to accompany five amphibious armored tractor personnel carriers on a special patrol. As the convoy lurched out of LZ Baldy the Marines sat atop the amtracs with their weapons ready for any action.

The vehicles lurched along making so much noise they drowned out any hope of conversation. Hathcock had a slight feeling that this wasn't the safest setting he would have chosen. No longer was he at home in his jungle. He felt a little too exposed where he was on number three amtrac in the middle of the group. A minesweeping team working ahead of the convoy gave them some sense of security. Still Carlos felt uneasy. Any operation as noisy and tempting as this attracted too much attention.

As the armored transports turned one by one off the road onto a gravel trail that a patrol had followed days earlier, his vehicle triggered a 500-pound box mine causing a thunderous explosion that erupted in a 40-foot high wall of smoke and flames engulfing Hathcock and the seven other Marines with him. Fifty other marines in the convoy scrambled for cover as rapid rifle fire from a nearby tree line told them they had stumbled into an ambush.

When he regained consciousness he felt all wet. It was fuel and he was on fire! In the blazing vehicle all Carlos could think of was to grab the burning bodies he saw around him and get them out of this fiery hell as quickly as possible. He went back again and again to drag them out of this hell, unmindful of the fact that he was a walking bomb himself with a cartridge-belt full of ammunition and six hand grenades hanging from his flaming webbing. He was so stunned from it all that he tried not to look at his burned arms with skin looped down and burning even as he pulled yet another Marine off the vehicle. Then his legs gave out on him and he dropped into a pool of cool water alongside the gravel road and mercifully lost any feeling of pain as he blacked out.

Everything that happened after that was pretty much a blur. He remembered a medic asking him to drink canteen after canteen of water which he did, then everyone was working to get the burned men air-lifted to hospitals as soon as they could. Another chopper carried him and seven other seriously burned Marines to the Da Nang Air Force Base where they were put aboard a jet for Tokyo. Hathcock never knew how long he stayed at those hospitals along the way nor did he remember that they worked with him and the others at the world famous burn center at the Brook Army Base at San Antonio, Texas.

Slowly but surely Carlos Hathcock recovered from the second and third degree burns he had over 43 percent of his body. Jo, his wife went to him when he was being helped at the San Antonio burn center where he proudly showed her the Purple Heart medal that he had personally received from General Simpson.

"He commands the whole division," said Carlos, "and he came to see *me*." He was overwhelmed with pride and Jo choked down tears when she realized how much that meant to her husband.

Carlos went through thirteen operations where doctors removed his burned flesh and replaced it with skin grafts. But the pain, hallucinations and bad dreams and multiple infections never let up on him.

One of his officers who knew what happened wanted to recommend Carlos for a medal but he strongly objected to it, saying he had only done what anyone would have done under those circumstances. So instead the officer presented him with a mug engraved with all of his fellow Marines' names and he was pleased with that.

Over the coming months he had to protect himself from the sun from top to bottom. He wore gloves and a large hat. He wanted to get back into rifle shooting competition again but his body was too tender to stand up to the rigors that activity involved. In 1972 the Marine Corps transferred him to Camp Lejeune, North Carolina where he became one of the finest rifle–team coaches the Corps ever had. But he still could not shoot and was bothered by dizzy spells. The doctors said his problems were all tied to his severe burns.

Returning to Service where he was urged by Major Jim Land and others, Carlos joined them in establishing a special training school for snipers. Their Scout/Sniper School at the Marine base in Quantico, Virginia became a tremendous success.

In time however Carlos' health deteriorated and doctors finally diagnosed him with Multiple Sclerosis, a debilitating disease of the central nervous system for which there is no known cure. Carlos retired from the Marines with 100 percent disability.

At his retirement ceremony, he was given a plaque with a bronzed Marine campaign cover mounted above a brass plate that reads: "There have been many Marines. There have been many marksmen. But there has only been one sniper — Gunnery Sergeant Carlos N. Hathcock II. One Shot. One Kill." And eventually he was awarded The Silver Star, officially the Silver Star Medal, which is the third-highest military decoration for valor awarded to members of the United States Armed Forces. Any uniformed service-member may receive the medal, which is awarded for gallantry in action against an enemy of the United States.

HERE ARE HIS AWARDS AND CITATIONS

Silver Star

Awarded for actions during the Vietnam War

The President of the United States of America takes pleasure in presenting the Silver Star to Staff Sergeant Carlos N. Hathcock, II (MCSN: 1873109), United States Marine Corps, for conspicuous gallantry and intrepidity in action while serving as a Sniper, Seventh Marines, First Marine Division, in connection with military operations against the enemy in the Republic of Vietnam on 16 September 1969. Staff Sergeant Hathcock was riding on an Assault Amphibious Vehicle which ran over and detonated an enemy anti-tank mine, disabling the vehicle which was immediately engulfed in flames. He and other Marines who were riding on top of the vehicle were sprayed with flaming gasoline caused by the explosion. Although suffering from severe burns to his face, trunk, and arms and legs, Staff Sergeant Hathcock assisted the injured Marines in exiting the burning vehicle and moving to a place of relative safety. With complete disregard for his own safety and while suffering excruciating pain from his burns, he bravely ran back through the flames and exploding ammunition to ensure that no Marines had been left behind in the burning vehicle. His heroic actions were instrumental in saving the lives of several Marines. By his courage, aggressive leadership, and total devotion to duty in the face of extreme personal danger, Staff Sergeant Hathcock reflected great credit upon himself and the Marine Corps and upheld the highest traditions of the United States Naval Service.
Action Date: September 16, 1969

Service: Marine Corps

Rank: Staff Sergeant

Company: Sniper

Regiment: 7th Marines

Division: 1st Marine Division (Rein.), FMF

Hathcock's Virginia Beach, Virginia home became a Mecca for visiting friends and admirers. Carlos and his wife Jo welcomed them one and all. The walls of their modest home were lined with mementos of his illustrious shooting career, his photographs and awards. And I am sure he and Jo were enormously pleased with their son, Carlos Norman Hathcock III who had followed his father's footsteps into the Marines to serve a distinguished career in his own right.

And interestingly, Carlos started a new activity that gave him a taste of that fighting spirit he missed – sport fishing for large sharks. He and his shark-fishing buddies spent hours rigging their heavy equipment, then having friendly competitions as to who could fight and beach the largest shark. Carlos was especially proud of the fact that he had fought, bested and beached a large lemon shark weighing several hundred pounds. It's interesting that the camaraderie among shark fisherman in those years was similar to the camaraderie among combat soldiers. They were both engaged in a dangerous activity where if you are strong and capable you could rid the world of dangerous predators, while getting the same kind of excitement and high adrenalin rush common to combat soldiers, especially snipers. Coupled with all the friends and admirers who sought him out in the last years of his life and supported by his awards including the Silver Star it is good to know that the old warrior still enjoyed the fight to the very end.

QUOTES, RECOLLECTIONS AND TRIBUTES

[From the author, Robert F. Burgess] It's good to remember that the unique Marine snipers of the past were the ones who pioneered what sniping has evolved to today in all of its wondrous electronic wizardry. Back then in the mid-1960s it was a totally new learning experience. It was the real beginning of modern day sniping. When you consider what kind of equipment they had to work with, and how well some of them used those weapons to perform legendary feats, then we owe them all a major debt of gratitude. Those few who survived what they did, or perhaps didn't survive it, they all astounded us with their feats. They will always be our heroes. Over the years and into other wars these improvements have made the art of sniping much easier and safer for snipers to achieve their tasks. But modern sniping today with all of its electronic magic takes all the challenge and human initiative out of what snipers had to do in the past. To me the Golden Age of sniping occurred in the jungles of Vietnam in the mid-1960s.

But then I'm from the old school. Reading responses from latter-day snipers in Vietnam saying such things as "No Marine sniper was ever allowed to go out on a mission alone," or as a reviewer of one of my Vietnam sniper stories wrote: "Characters believable and good mix...few errors. No weapons in Nam chambered in .30-06." I scratch my head and wonder what planet these guys are from. In those early years they did indeed go out alone. And the weapon of choice they carried was the Winchester Model 70 .30-06.

Who better to represent these early Marine sniper heroes than the U.S. Marine's own Carlos Norman Hathcock II? Much has already been written about Carlos, but when these things are written a lot of details have to be left out. Some of these details are important because they shaped the kind of person he became. And they weren't always good things. On the contrary most of them were bad, or sad, whichever way you choose to consider them. Oddly it seems that the more difficult a time the young have in their early years, the better characters they become in their later years. Ernest Hemingway said, "We are stronger in the places that are broken."

That always seems to be true. If Carlos Hathcock were born into a wealthy inner-city environment where he was given whatever he wanted, I doubt that we would have heard anything about his sniper prowess in Vietnam. On the contrary for him it was just the opposite. So he became the legend. Below are some of the reasons why:

As one reporter described him, "He was the original laconic, cool-headed country boy. When put to the big-city test, he broke records. In those days, the Marine Corps wouldn't take anyone under 17. So, on his 17th birthday in 1959, Hathcock enlisted. During recruit training in San Diego, he immediately qualified as an expert with the M1 rifle, a .30-06 that was used widely by Marines and Army soldiers during WW II. It was a heavy rifle, and he could hit the 18-inch-diameter bull's-eye from 500 yards at the rifle range time after time. He developed a complete fascination with developing the skill and precision of long-range shooting with high-powered rifles. That fascination stayed with him the rest of his life."

******

"It was the stalk that I enjoyed," Carlos once told a reporter for the Washington Post. "Pitting yourself against another human being, there was no second place in Vietnam - second place was a body bag. Everybody was scared and those that say they weren't are liars. But you can let that work for you. It makes you more alert, keener, and that's how it got for me. It made me be the best."

******

After the war, a friend showed Hathcock this passage written by Ernest Hemingway: "Certainly there is no hunting like the hunting of man, and those who have hunted armed men long enough and like it, never really care for anything else thereafter."

Hathcock copied Hemingway's words on a piece of paper. "He got that right," Hathcock said. "It was the hunt, not the killing."

******

Another reporter wrote: "Before he was stricken with MS, Hathcock was unmatched in his ability to endure physical and mental hardships to position himself for a kill. With the slow, deliberate moves of a panther in the night, Hathcock would stalk his targets sometimes for days and inches at a time."

******

Carlos felt that a good sniper needed seven characteristics to get the job done and get back to base alive. According to the list, a sniper must be an excellent marksman, a good woodsman, emotionally stable so as not to be easily excited, smart and keenly observant, aware of his surroundings, good with a map and compass and patient.

"It takes an awareness of the environment and total concentration at the moment you fire the shot. You have to be aware of the wind, which has a tremendous impact at 1,000 yards; you have to be aware of the sun, whether it goes behind a cloud or not. Then, at the last millisecond, if you will, you have to develop total concentration.

It takes a tremendous amount of discipline," Marine Major Edward Land who trained Carlos said. He noted that while most other Marine snipers were proficient or above average in their skills, Hathcock's uncanny abilities took him to another level entirely.

"The thing that made him different in Vietnam, it wasn't the marksmanship skill, but he just had this ability to totally integrate himself into the environment, and he noticed everything. He had a total awareness of his surroundings," Land said. "We all developed an edge, but Carlos took it one step further. He was like a mountain man. He noticed every breeze, every insect. He certainly did have Indian blood."

Often, Land said, a sniper would have to sit for long periods totally still and silent. If the enemy was near, any movement could mean instant death. "A lot of times you would be sitting so long in one place you either urinated or defecated in your trousers," he said.

The bush could be very unpleasant after several days of no bathing, getting bitten by ants and mosquitoes, going without food and water, the basics. Once, while on a mission, Hathcock came face to face with a deadly snake. But because the Viet Cong were close by, he could not move. He had to stare at the snake and pray. After several tense minutes, the snake flicked its tongue and slithered into the underbrush.

He once said that he survived in his work because of an ability to "get in the bubble," to put himself into a state of "utter, complete, absolute concentration," first on his equipment, then on his environment in which every breeze and every leaf meant something, and finally on his quarry.

"Carlos became part of the environment," said Edward Land, Hathcock's commanding officer who often accompanied Carlos as his spotter. "He totally integrated himself into the environment. He had the patience, drive, and courage to do the job. He felt very strongly that he was saving Marine lives." With 93 confirmed kills – his longest was at 2500 yards – and an estimated 300 more, for Hathcock, it really wasn't about the killing.

"I really didn't like the killing," he once told a reporter.

"You'd have to be crazy to enjoy running around the woods, killing people. But if I didn't get the enemy, they were going to kill the kids over there." Saving American lives is something Hathcock took to heart.

For four days and three nights, he low-crawled inch by inch, a move he called "worming," without food or sleep, more than 1500 yards to get close to the general. This was the only time he ever removed the feather from his cap. "Over a time period like that you could forget the strategy, forget the rules and end up dead," Carlos said. "I didn't want anyone dead, so I took the mission myself, figuring I was better than the rest of them, because I was training them."

******

In 1990 a Marine unit raised $5,000 in donations to fight multiple sclerosis and presented it to him at his home. They brought it to him the old-fashioned way, the Marine way: They ran 216 miles from Camp Lejune, N.C., to Virginia Beach.

It was a tribute to his toughness that Carlos Hathcock understood.

According to the account in the Norfolk Virginian-Pilot, the old sniper told the men, "I am so touched, I can hardly talk."

******

In an in-depth article John Feamster wrote for *Precision Shooting* in March, 1996, these excerpts from his interview provide a glimpse of his home life and what this author had to say about his first meeting with the legendary Carlos Hathcock II:

Now, eight years after reading his story, I was finally to have a chance to meet the man behind the legend! As I parked my rental car in front of a neat, red brick house in Virginia Beach, Virginia, it became apparent that I had found the right place. On this sunny, fall day - appropriately enough, the Marine Corps birthday - American and USMC flags fluttered from a mast in the front yard.

A late-model pickup, scrupulously clean, bore the custom license plate, "SNIPER". Then, the hard reality of Carlos' illness hit home when I saw the well-built wheelchair ramp and handrail leading to the front door. And, finally, there was Carlos Hathcock himself, smiling pleasantly as he walked to greet me. My first impression was almost exactly what I'd expected. A slender man, with a trim, athletic build and a firm handshake despite his ongoing battle with multiple sclerosis, Carlos wore crisp blue jeans, a neat shirt, spit-shined shoes and, ever the Marine, a fresh haircut. As he ushered me into a comfortable living room filled with knickknacks, family photos and mementos of his Marine service, whatever trepidation I might have felt was soon put to rest. Outside, the autumn wind rustled a few leaves in the yard as I settled on the couch and we got acquainted.

Carlos' cat, Buddy, a huge and affectionate feline, purred contentedly on the arm of the sofa as I scratched his ears, while Lady, their dog, lay by the door anticipating Mrs. Hathcock's return from the grocery store. Before long, it was lunchtime and Carlos and I repaired to the Open House diner near his home, where he is one of the regulars. Over an old-fashioned meal of waffles, eggs and (of course) grits, he put me at ease as we swapped stories about hunting and shooting… "…I kept my scopes zeroed at 700 yards!" Would a more modern rifle have made much difference in Hathcock's effectiveness? "Yes! Definitely! We had wood stocks, which didn't do very well over there - the zero kept changing. A fiberglass stock would have kept our zeros the same."

Carlos mentioned that he had not used the M-21 (accurized M-14 sniper system) while overseas. How about suppressors? "No, our noise suppressor was distance. We just shot from so far away they couldn't tell where we were." Did Hathcock ever use night vision? "No, I never did. Now, I did use an infrared scope one night, and I was scanning with this scope, and there was an infrared looking back at me! Click! I turned that sucker off quick! It was an attention-getter! We never really had much night vision capability with our rifles, anyhow.

Starlight wasn't too much good. You could kill the heck out of a tombstone, and all you gotta do is pay for it." He laughed as he explained, "McAbee did that - he saw this tombstone that looked just like one of the bad guys... he kept banging at it, but it never fell, and he had to pay for it. I didn't like them Starlights, anyway. Things were green in there, and I never could make anything out with 'em, to tell you the truth."

What was Carlos' opinion of the standard M-14 rifle in combat? "It was very reliable... very, VERY reliable. When them M-16's first came in country, man, they were killin' a lot of people - the people shootin' 'em! When I went back the second time, I would NOT let my people carry the M-16 'cause I wanted all my people to come back. And, I never lost a person over there." He laughed good-naturedly as he went on, "Never lost nobody but me, and that wasn't my fault!" What does Carlos think of the M-16 now, with all the improvements that have been made to it since Viet Nam? "Well, I've never had much experience with M-16's. My son [SSG Carlos N. Hathcock III, USMC] seems to like it, 'cause that's what he's armed with. He shoots it in matches, and he seems to like it."

Carlos mentioned that he had kept his rifle zeroed at 700 yards while in Viet Nam. I was especially curious as to whether he might have worked out a trajectory table for his scope in clicks per 100 yards, in order to change his elevation zero as needed. "No, I mainly held off, and I taught my people in my platoon to hold off, too." How much wind did he encounter in Viet Nam? "It was considerable. I was shooting across a river, one time, and the wind just whistled down the river. I missed two bad guys in one day... I didn't hold off, and hit in front of both of 'em. Then, other times, I held just right..."

How about in the early mornings and late evenings? "Oh, yeah, it was calmer then, except in the monsoon season, when it was windy all the time. It was rainy... Jeez, what a time that was." Could he operate effectively during the monsoon season? "No, that's when you turned into an observer, actually...."

As our interview drew to a close, I asked Carlos, "If you could tell the competitive shooters anything that you think would be of value to them, what would it be?" His answer was succinct: "Stay off drugs and keep training. Practice, practice, practice. If you want to be any good at all, you've got to practice. I never did want to be no 'used-to-was'! You being a shooter yourself, you know that shooting is a deteriorating skill... if you don't stay in practice, you'll lose it!" And, what would Carlos like to convey to military and police snipers today? "Maintain your discipline - physical and mental. That will carry you over; you've got to have discipline in everything you do out there. In the police aspect, especially, if you don't have discipline, you're in left field - you'll get sued. That's the big thing today, is to sue somebody. The shot that you make has to be the correct shot. That's where discipline comes in, and careful, extensive observation. You don't want to risk shooting the hostage, thinking he's the bad guy."

TOWARD THE END

These days, Carlos Hathcock can no longer hunt or shoot. It is obviously a matter of sincere regret to him that he can no longer instruct police marksmen, due to his advancing illness. His enduring love of teaching is manifest. When talking about marksmanship principles or the need for discipline, the fire and drive that led him to his remarkable achievements appears, and the Hathcock of old emerges. It is typical of the man. Whatever he does, he does one hundred percent. Today, Carlos has few, if any, other interests, and his illness has stolen his chief pleasures in life. Despite his losses - or, perhaps in small part, because of them - the shooting fraternity continues to stand by him, as I saw during my visits.

Carlos and his wife, Jo, receive frequent calls from shooters, soldiers and veterans, wishing them well, and Carlos reports that this helps him. The Hathcocks have made many friends during their travels. Throughout their house, one notices plaques and awards that attest to the respect and appreciation Carlos has earned through his selfless contributions to law enforcement, the military, and the shooting community at large.

It is vital not to overlook the sacrifices Carlos Hathcock made in the service of his country. Of course, he faced danger, physical hardships and separation from his family as a professional soldier. These are the risks that soldiers take, and Carlos accepted them as part of his chosen career. As a shooter, however, he gave all. In 1965, he was nearing the peak of his shooting ability, having won the Wimbledon Cup and having only narrowly missed taking the National Service Rifle Championship. He did this as a relatively new competitor!

There can be little doubt that he had the skill, the drive, the determination and the potential to be a national champion many times over. Horribly burned during his second tour of duty in Viet Nam, Carlos' physical limitations would never permit him to achieve his full potential as a competitor, and he misses shooting to this very day.

Now, the camaraderie of the shooting fraternity constitutes one of his few remaining pleasures. Jo Hathcock, too, deserves special recognition for her steadfast nature. Life as the bride of Carlos Hathcock cannot have been easy, at times. From her early days as a "shooting widow" when Carlos was competing on the Marine team, to the months of uncertainty about his safety when he served in Viet Nam, to helping him through the lengthy recovery from his burns and his later adjustment to multiple sclerosis, Jo Hathcock has always been there. Now, although experiencing significant health problems of her own, Jo graciously greets her husband's many admirers, and accepts without complaints the frequent interruptions to her otherwise quiet life. Carlos and Jo are a matched pair - they are dependable.

When I traveled to meet Carlos Hathcock, he was frozen in my mind's eye as an almost supernatural figure - a lean, fit young Marine, keen of eye, the epitome of stealth and cunning - as still and patient as Death itself. Like a wraith, he stalked the jungle, melting into it and making it his own, much like its native tiger. Certainly, Carlos has become an icon to many in the shooting world - a symbol of what one may achieve through skill, self-discipline and courage. And, it is safe to say that as long as the old-fashioned virtues of patriotism, self-sacrifice, skill at arms and bravery exist, Carlos Hathcock will be remembered. However, what I observed as I got to know him was courage of a different sort.

This was not so much the gallantry of a soldier on the battlefield, but the quiet resolution of a man fighting to gracefully manage an illness that he can't control, and which he knows must someday, inexorably, overwhelm him, despite his best efforts. This is the calm, steady courage born of strength of character which enables Carlos Hathcock to endure pain 24 hours a day without complaint, and to think of others and their welfare even when living a desperate, daily battle of his own. In the final analysis, both Carlos and Jo Hathcock impressed me as simple, honest, goodhearted folks. Life tries them daily, and they are not found wanting. Carlos is aware of his fame, but routinely dismisses his heroic actions a bit self-consciously, saying, "I was just doing my job." As he said when I left for home, "We're just people."

My time in Virginia Beach was especially meaningful to me. I had the opportunity to express my appreciation to Carlos Hathcock for all that he did for his country, which I have long wanted to do. But, there was an unexpected bonus, as well. When I walked up the driveway to that neat, little house in Virginia, I shook hands with a legend. Through Carlos' pleasant, open nature, when I left, I shook hands with a friend.

Author's note: The contents and accuracy of this article were approved by Carlos Hathcock.Nathaniel Hathcock III

(The following appeared on an Internet Marine website)

Tuesday 23 February 1999
It is with great sadness that I must inform you that retired Marine sniper GySgt. Carlos left us this morning at 0630. Carlos went into the hospital last week with a kidney infection and was supposed to come home on Friday 26 February. Carlos suffered from MS, and for the past two years had been confined to home and bed.
Those who did not know this man, missed out on a great gentle and caring person who without reservation gave all for his country.
God bless you Carlos, rest in peace.

All the major newspapers across America carried his obituary along with major articles about this American hero's exploits. Excerpts from two of them that appeared on the Internet are here.

On 28 Feb 1999, Los Angeles Times Staff Writer Jon Thurber wrote in part:
"His vanity license plates in Virginia read SNIPER, and during the Vietnam War he was just that, the bearer of a surprising, sudden death to enemy soldiers. But when Marine Gunnery Sgt. Carlos N. Hathcock II died last week at the age of 57, the enemy that ultimately felled him was the slow, patient progression of multiple sclerosis."

******

A representative of a local Native American tribe was invited to Hathcock's funeral, and he presented eagle feathers to Hathcock's wife, Jo; his son, Carlos III; and Hathcock's shooting buddy, Jim Land. The Indians respected this lone warrior, who was part Indian.

Carlos Hathcock Encounters

"I met Mr. Hathcock at the Waukesha Rifle and Pistol Associations banquet a few years back. Before he spoke, he walked around, meeting the rifle and pistol competitors that were in attendance (about 600 of us showed up), talking and shaking hands. Then he came by our table. Carlos is one of those guys that you expect to be about seven feet tall, and figuratively, he was! I stood up to shake his hand and say hello, and towering over him I felt compelled to sit back down. You just don't feel right being taller than this legend! He shook my hand, asked about the firearms that I shoot in competition, and handed me his card. When he finally got up on the podium to speak, and tell the stories, and answer questions, you would have been amazed at the amount of noise that 600 people made...none! I didn't hear a single chair squeak, or a throat get cleared, nothing but pure silence. This was truly a living legend we all met that day, and he couldn't have been a nicer more down to earth guy. Semper-Fi Gunny!" -- Mike H. (15aug98)

"About 6 months ago I was on aol, talking in the Marines' chat room. A couple of guys were on and questioned me about the M40A1. I answered their questions. They gave me Carlos Hathcock's personal phone number. I was a little leery about calling him, but I did. Talk about a complete gentleman and always a Marine. He took my call, I explained that I was also a Marine Corps Sniper and we talked for about 30 minutes.

Mostly about the Corps. I understand he has been put in for a Silver Star. I hope he gets it. Carlos loves to hear from fellow snipers. -- Robert C. (8july98)

"...Since that time in Quantico, all three of us have completed the course in Virginia Beach...and guess who met us at the door..."Gunny" Funny thing, he remembered me and before I could introduce myself he asked, "Stopped your heart lately?" I was floored! I will be forever grateful to "Gunny" for passing on his knowledge and experience to each of us. The training he provided has helped to save lives not merely take them. Carlos Hathcock gave us instruction that made us think of not only of the shot but about discipline and patience." [Author's Note: Carlos taught his snipers how to concentrate on slowing down their heartbeat so they would be calm when they shot. He recognized James as one of his trainees hence the heart-stopping remark.] -- James C. (SA-FBI) (7oct98)

"...It was against our better judgment to bother him before his meal. But we knew it would be our only chance to meet him. He was patient, polite and extremely courteous. I was amazed at his demeanor. He is one very pleasant gentleman. He is a hero and we let him know how much we appreciated what he did. After our conversation and a photo shoot...which didn't come out, we retreated to our booth. The gentleman that was with him came to our booth and asked if we were Marines. We weren't and told him our story. My cousin's husband was active Army at the time and I was prior Army. He said Carlos was very impressed. Not many Marines know who he is, much less recognize him. He handed us both a gold business card with a sniper rifle and a feather on it." --Eric Q. (14oct98)

"...Not only that, but I found he lived very close by and as fate would have it I was prodding the isles of a gun show in Hampton VA, when I happened to glance to my right and look into the eyes of a face I knew well: Gunny Hathcock. And not only did I get to shake his hand but got an autographed photo to boot. What a day!" -- William L. (5Dec98)

"...Carlos and I shot together at Cherry Point in the early '60s and had a lot of fun kidding the other shooters about being "Yankees". Carlos broke my long-standing qualification course record there and liked to kid me about it....but I never forgot Ol' Carlos and his snicky giggle and was real proud of calling him my friend." -- Captain William E."Doc" L. USMC (Retired) (19feb99)

"...I shook his hand and chatted with him while he ate a bowl of ice cream ... I just felt good sitting in his presence. I couldn't think of any great ballistic or gun questions. After about 5 minutes I excused myself letting the guy finish his treat in peace. He was a true hero and gentleman." -- Mike O. (25feb99)

"...I was very surprised when I met him, he put everyone immediately at ease, his knowledge of shooting was unmatched. I learned more from that one week of training than I had from any of the other training I had ever attended combined. He was definitely a professional and a gentleman. A true Marine. He will be greatly missed. America has lost one of its greatest heroes." -- Mike G. (26feb99)

"I was a member of the Coast Guard Pistol Team when he came out to the range at Dam Neck, VA during the All Navy Matches. We listened to him talk for an hour or so while he graciously wished us luck and signed our score books..." -- GM1 Mike C., USCG (24dec99)

"My father was one of Gunny's students @ Quantico in the late 70's. He has always spoke truly of Gunny and the way he would be able to yell at you without even saying a word. I wanted badly to meet this man since I was little and it finally happened when I was about 9 yrs. old. Gunny came to stay with us at my house for a week when he came up to Maryland to help my dad with the sniper school he was instructing for the police dept. Every night at dinner we would all sit around and listen to stories Gunny had to talk about. I do have to say…There was never a dull moment when he was around. Ever since that week, I have been in close contact with Gunny all the way up to his death. He was even generous enough to send me a new 50 dollar bill for graduation. Talk about someone who revels in the likings of youngsters. He was a great man and will always be in the heart of me and my family. My father still cries when he thinks of how Gunny used to tell him to put himself in his "own little bubble" when he was shooting. Thanks for the advice Gunny and thanks to you…" -- Brian B. (20apr99)

"…I went to the infamous marine PMI school. (Primary Marksmanship Instructor), and Carlos spoke at our graduation. It was the most memorable moment of my 7 years in the marines. When he entered the room in his wheel chair, you could hear a pin drop. The whole entire audience was afraid to look at him. He got out of his wheel chair and walked slowly up to the microphone, and then he started talking about how much he hated people that spit their chewing gum on the street. The whole audience started to crack up. And he kept going on and on and on about how he had to pull it off the bottom of his shoes….

"He spoke to us for about 30 minutes even though he was in serious pain. And when he was finished, he stayed after graduation to chat with his fellow marines, autograph books, and have his photo taken with us.
Semper Fi, Carlos" -- Sgt. Gregory P. M. 1stBn 2ndMar A Co. 2nd MarDiv (19oct2000)

"So, with no idea at all what to say to him, I called. I simply asked, "May I speak to Carlos Hathcock?" He said, "This is he." I replied with…"I hope this isn't gonna sound crazy, but are you the soldier who was the inspiration for the book *Marine Sniper*? He paused for a terrifying few seconds, and said, "I am he." The only thing I could do was to say how much I admired him, and that I enjoyed the book. He came back with a statement that made me speechless. He said…"You have got some nerve calling me."…I immediately got sick in my stomach. Then he said, "But I love a person with a lot of nerve, come meet me, and have lunch!" He didn't have to ask twice. We talked for about 30 minutes on the phone, and he gave me his home address, which was about 10 minutes from where I lived.

He acted like he had known me for years. He and his wife were as sweet as anyone could ever imagine…" -- Donna H-G. (18aug2001)

"I first met Carlos while in the Marine Corps back in 1984 my first year as a young Marine Sgt. assigned to the Marine Corps Rifle Team in Quantico, Va. I had heard stories about the famous Marine Sniper. I remember first seeing him, he was a small-framed guy. I introduced myself to him. He was barely able to move around due to his illness. He was wearing the coveted Marine Corps shooting jacket given to all Marines who are fortunate to make it to the big team. Looking in his eyes was amazing! He was very pleasant and loved to talk about the conditions of shooting! I was in awe! I had the pleasure of shooting along side of his son a couple of years later. Carlos will be missed greatly however he will never be forgotten by this former Marine." -- Thomas C. (21apr2004)

And finally, this touching tribute from a comrade at arms.

For Carlos...

Carlos is gone... Somehow, it just doesn't seem possible! I think I had begun to think of him as indestructible! It seems like only yesterday that I was standing behind him in a line to get our triggers weighed prior to shooting the Division Matches at Camp Lejeune in the early 60s. I've shot with him, soldiered with him and been his OIC and Commanding Officer, and he never once failed to do his job brilliantly, or disappointed me in any way. For all of his expertise as a sniper, for all of his heroism, for all of his shooting ability, I think I will remember him most for his sense of humor and willingness to help others – his other accomplishments are a matter of history.

He was a man of great personal accomplishments, who never quite realized that he was a celebrity in his own right. Any attempt to heap praise on him resulted in his hanging his head and dragging his toe in the dirt. Not that he didn't realize that he knew his stuff with a rifle at his shoulder he just was not comfortable in the spotlight. He was the original, All-American reluctant hero, who never quite saw anything heroic in his deeds... It took the rest of us to promote his brilliance, if left to his own devices, Carlos would have remained an unknown Marine who did his job and did it exceptionally well!

Everything in me makes me want to recount his amazing deeds and accomplishments, but that's been done before in many places, and this isn't meant to be a history, just a good-bye to an old friend.

Carlos is not really gone however. As long as there are those of us who keep him alive in our hearts and memories, he will never die. As long as there is a Marine Corps, Carlos' memory will always be alive. His legacy of self-sacrifice and heroism will always serve as an inspiration to those who follow in his footsteps. As long as there is a place in our hearts for decency and honor and bravery, Carlos will live. May it always be so.

In Norse mythology, fallen heroes were welcomed to Valhalla as a reward for valorous conduct. Those of us in the profession of arms often speak of this, the warriors' final resting-place, where no one grows old, and honor is held in high esteem. If there is an all-knowing and all-wise God, as there must surely be, we will someday meet Carlos at the gates of Valhalla... I only hope that we will be as worthy of entrance to those hallowed halls as the immortal "White Feather."

So here's one last toast to Carlos. Lift your glasses to heroism, self-sacrifice, and devotion to duty in the face of extreme adversity. To my old friend, until we meet again.

Semper Fi,
Dick Culver

End Note:

This was written on the morning Carlos passed on to Valhalla. While we had all known that his end was inevitable, I suppose that somewhere down deep, he had become a symbol of a transition era within our sacred Corps of Marines, and that somehow Carlos would always be there when you needed him. Much like the legendary Captain Jimmy Bones who tended the gates of Hell, we have always suspected that when needed most, Carlos will take the necessary leave from his duties in Odin's Great Hall. The guides to Valhalla are known as the Valkyries who chose only the most valiant warriors and escorted them to their place of honor. Certainly they could have made no better choice than Carlos. Those chosen are welcomed by Odin's son, Bragi, the master of the spoken word and noted for his poetic excellence. In Carlos' case, his lexicon may have been overwhelmed by a most unique individual who quite possibly may have caused Bragi to exceed his normal eloquence.

ABOUT THE AUTHOR

At the end of World War II, the author who was attached to Charlie Company First Battalion 351st Infantry Regiment of the 88th Blue Devil Division Ski Troops served in northern Italy bringing out German POWs from fortified mountains in the Italian Alps. The army rated him Expert with the M1 Garand rifle. His outfit later became TRUST the first Trieste U.S. Troops to permanently occupy disputed territory between Italy and Yugoslavia, which included the important port of Trieste on the Adriatic. His garrison in 1946 turned back Marshal Tito and his army who were determined to take Trieste. Later that disputed territory became part of Italy.

Robert F. Burgess resides in North Florida. His other books and short stories can be found on **Amazon.com**.

Other Books by Robert F. Burgess Available at Amazon.com

1. To Majorca With Love
2. Real Cliffhangers
3. Hemingway's Paris and Pamplona, Then and Now
4. Meeting Hemingway in Pamplona
5. Florida's Golden Galleons
6. Secret World Of The Sharks
7. Lone Wolf of the Wolfhounds
8. Secrets Of A Happy Hooker
9. Ghost Sniper
10. Return Of The Ghost Sniper
11. Revenge Of The Ghost Sniper
12. The Sweet Goodbye
13. Zapping The Zebra
14. Two For The Marquesas
15. Diving To Adventure
16. Sailing To Adventure
17. Find More Treasure
18. How They Escaped
19. Diving Into The Past
20. They Found Treasure
21. Fire, Ice And Inca Gold
22. Catch More Lobsters
23. Finding Sunken Treasure
24. 1715 Treasure
25. Tracking Treasure By Computer
26. One Night On Scarborough Pond
27. Sniper Up!
28. Charlie, You're Not Perfect
29. Rolling Thunder
30. Carlos Hathcock's Longest Mission
31. Mystery Snipers, CIA Wizardry, and Our Fight against Isis
32. Charlie Brown Sniper

Made in the USA
Columbia, SC
19 March 2024